ALGERNON CHARLES SWINBURNE

A Study

BY

THEODORE WRATISLAW

London

GREENING & CO., LTD.

20 CECIL COURT, CHARING CROSS ROAD

1900

DATE DUE FOR R

a

ALGERNON CHARLES SWINBURNE

ALGERNON CHARLES SWINBURNE.

CONTENTS

	PAGE
PROLOGUE, ...	I
UNDERGRADUATE PAPERS (1858), ...	7
THE QUEEN-MOTHER AND ROSAMUND (1860), . .	8
DEAD LOVE (1864), ...	II

THE POEMS

ATALANTA IN CALYDON (1865), ...	15
CHASTELARD (1865), ...	24
POEMS AND BALLADS—FIRST SERIES (1866), . . .	36
SONGS BEFORE SUNRISE (1871), ...	55
BOTHWELL (1874), ...	67
SONGS OF TWO NATIONS (1875), ...	68
ERECTHEUS (1876), ...	68
POEMS AND BALLADS—SECOND SERIES (1878), . .	74
SONGS OF THE SPRINGTIDES (1880), ...	85
STUDIES IN SONG (1880), ...	89
MARY STUART (1881), ...	94
TRISTRAM OF LYONESSE (1882), ...	97
A CENTURY OF ROUNDELS (1882), ...	109

PAGE

A Midsummer Holiday (1884), ... 112

Marino Faliero (1885), ... 115

Locrine (1887), ... 122

Poems and Ballads—Third Series (1889), . . . 125

The Sisters (1892), ... 137

Astrophel and Other Poems (1894), ... 142

The Tale of Balen (1896), ... 147

Rosamund, Queen of the Lombards (1899), . . 148

THE PROSE WORKS

Notes on Poems and Reviews (1866), . . . 153

William Blake (1868), ... 154

Under the Microscope (1872), ... 154

Essays and Studies (1875), ... 155

George Chapman (1865), ... 165

Charlotte Brontë (1877), ... 165

A Study of Shakespeare (1880), ... 166

A Study of Victor Hugo (1886), ... 173

Miscellanies (1886), ... 174

A Study of Ben Jonson (1889), ... 187

Studies in Prose and Poetry (1894), . . . 191

EPILOGUE, ... 200

APPENDIX, ... 209

SWINBURNE

PROLOGUE

ALGERNON CHARLES SWINBURNE, the eldest
child of Admiral Charles Henry Swinburne
and Lady Henrietta Jane, daughter of the
third Earl of Ashburnham, was born in
London on the 5th April 1837. Admiral
Swinburne, who was the second son of Sir
John Edward Swinburne, Baronet, died in
1877, Lady Henrietta Jane Swinburne
within the last few years.

'The very ancient family' of Swinburne,
says Burke, 'derived its name from Swinburne Castle in Northumberland, which it
possessed from so remote a period that
(although Sir William Dugdale notes them
not as such) the Swinburnes of Swinburne
Castle have been esteemed feudal lords.'

Swinburne Castle, however, passed away
from the family on the death of Adam de
Swinburne in the time of Edward II., with-

A

out male issue. The present family is descended from Sir William de Swinburne, who lived in the time of Henry III. The present baronet, Sir John Swinburne, is a first cousin of the poet. The family seat is Capheaton Castle in Northumberland.

The Swinburne baronetcy dates back to 1660, the barony of Ashburnham to 1689 and the earldom to 1730. The family of Ashburnham is, according to Nisbet, 'One of the ancientest families of good account before the Conquest.'

Of the personality and life of the poet little is known, and such accounts as have seen the light have been incorrect even when they have not been false. He was educated at Eton and Balliol, but he left Oxford without taking his degree—for the extraordinary reason, I understand, that, although he knew more Greek than his examiners, and more of most subjects than his co-examinees, he was 'ploughed' in 'Scripture,' which he had not taken the trouble to 'get up.' At Oxford he made the acquaintance of Dante Gabriel Rossetti

—who was then engaged in painting frescoes on the walls of the Union—and of Burne-Jones and Morris. Shortly after leaving Oxford, when he was staying with his family in Italy, he called with a letter of introduction on Walter Savage Landor, then in his last years. The admiration of the youngest for the oldest 'singer' of that time found expression in the dedication to Landor of the *Atalanta*, in excellent Greek verses. To the influence of his gifted mother, who was educated in Italy and taught the poet Italian, the affection of Swinburne for that southern country is no doubt due. His admiration for Victor Hugo began very early in life, not improbably dating from the time when he received a copy of *Notre Dame de Paris* as a school prize. The first time, however, that he saw Hugo was in November 1882, on the occasion of the revival in Paris of *Le Roi S'Amuse*. His early life was divided between Capheaton Castle in Northumberland, the seat of his grandfather, and East Dene at Bonchurch in the Isle of Wight, an estate which had been purchased by his father. Divided by a stone wall from the hillside road which runs northward past the old Bonchurch Churchyard, backed by the magnificent St Boniface Down, half enclosed by woods, but open in front to the fine sweep of pasturage which descends to the road overlooking the cliffs and the sea, the white rambling house of East Dene is a delightful pleasure-house to gaze upon. In the new churchyard at Bonchurch, a little higher on the cliff side, are the simple graves of the poet's father and mother. A few miles on the other side of Ventnor is the house named The Orchard, formerly the property of his uncle by marriage, Sir Henry Gordon, who was the husband of his aunt, Lady Mary Ashburnham. The road which leads from Ventnor to St Catherine's Point and Blackgang Chine runs below high downs and cliffs, and above a gentler slope of land descending to the sea, through a wooded district known as the Undercliff. Below this road in one spot is the estate and white house of The Orchard, perhaps more delightfully placed even than East Dene. Here also was the poet a frequent visitor. Many of Swinburne's most beautiful poems—for instance the *Forsaken Garden*—are inspired by the scenery of the Isle of Wight, and in the dedicatory verses to Lady Mary Gordon of *The Sisters* he recalls his early memories of The Orchard with its terraces of flowers, its 'shadowed lawns' and 'shadowing pines,' with its sun, its cliffs and its sea. Probably no poet has ever been so favoured by fortune in his early life in the matter of beautiful surroundings as well as the exemption from the necessity of labour in other fields than Art's. At a later date, after leaving Oxford and after a short stay on the Continent, he found the fascination of London. It was at this time that he shared for a year a house in Cheyne Walk, Chelsea, with Rossetti and Meredith. Thereafter he had chambers in London—in North Crescent, Great James Street and Guildford Street at various times. East Dene was sold after the death of a sister of the poet, and the headquarters of his nearest relatives then became Holmwood, near Reading. For the last twenty years the poet has lived on the edge of Wimbledon Common, sharing a house with his 'best friend,' Mr Theodore Watts-Dunton, and making an annual excursion with his friend to the seaside for his chief delight — swimming. His love of the sea and swimming is a prominent feature of his poetry. The well-known incident of his narrow escape from drowning, referred to once by himself in a poem, *Ex Voto*, occurred in his early manhood at Etretat in Normandy. He was carried away by a strong current and was luckily picked up by some fishermen.

The portrait by Watts of Swinburne as a young man is well known. The mass of reddish hair, the high forehead, aquiline nose and narrowing under face with a very slight moustache on the upper lip, are characteristics so often dwelt on that it may be permissible to repeat them. The curious resemblance between the early portraits of Swinburne and of M. Paderewski has been often noticed. Perhaps the best likenesses of the early Swinburne have been caught by his friend Rossetti, but the best photograph of the very few taken in recent years is reproduced in the front of this volume. At the present day Mr Swinburne, as he appeared to the present writer at a chance meeting, seems twenty years younger than his actual age, possessing still the animation which in his early manhood won him the name of 'boy poet,' and a manner of perfect courtesy.

The earliest known writings of Swinburne consist of three articles and a poem which appeared in 1858, in an Oxford publication, entitled *Undergraduate Papers*. They were entitled :—

Undergraduate Papers, 1858.

'The Early English Dramatists. No. 1. Marlowe and Fletcher.'

'The Monomaniac's Tragedy and other poems.' By Ernest Wheldrake. Author of 'Eve : a Mystery.' London 1858.'

'Church Imperialism.'

'Queen Yseult.' Canto 1. Of the birth of Sir Tristram and how he voyaged into Ireland.'

Of this publication, *Undergraduate Papers*, which was edited by Professor Nichol, only four copies are known to exist.

The title of the first article explains itself. The second was a (presumptively ironical) review of an imaginary book of poems, the quoted verses being by the hand of the reviewer. The third was an attack on the French Empire and its clerical supporters. The poem has since been re-written by its author.

In the titles and contents of these essays and this poem, published at the age of twenty-one, the beginning of the Swinburne that we know is obvious.

Two years later, in 1860, the poet, then The Queen- aged twenty-three, published his Mother and first book, *The Queen-Mother and* Rosamund, *Rosamund*, which has long been 1860. out of print. Of the two plays which make up the volume, the first, *The Queen-Mother*, is the longer and the more dramatic. It is, as it were, a prologue to the three plays which Swinburne in later years has devoted to the character of Mary

Queen of Scots. The Queen-Mother in question is Catherine de Medici, and the play is laid in the time of the Massacre of St Bartholomew. Among its characters are Charles IX. of France, Henry of Navarre and his wife Margaret, the authoress of the *Heptameron*, and Henry, Duke of Guise. It was in the court of Queen Catherine that Mary Stuart was reared, 'in the atmosphere of a palace which,' the dramatist wrote at a later date, 'it would be flattery to call a brothel or a slaughter-house.' The principal interest of the play is historic, and the horror of the time is well suggested.

The nascent cleverness of the writing of the play is as clear as its immaturity. The weakness of its immaturity, however, is as strong as the strength of many a would-be dramatist, and the undertone of its writer's poetic temperament is evident. The style appears to a certain extent to be founded on Shakespeare, but much of the later Swinburne is visible here.

Such a phrase as—

'The sea's yellow and distempered foam,'

for instance, recalls both Shakespeare and Swinburne.

The little play of *Rosamund*, the mistress of Henry II. and of Woodstock, is written in five short scenes. Its verbiage is more elaborate, more designedly poetic, than that of its predecessor. Here and there are traces of the influence of Browning, but there is much more in it of the Swinburne of the later *Chastelard* and *Poems and Ballads* than the critics of the poem would have one believe. The play is curiously uneven. At first Rosamund is represented as a somewhat proud type of beauty.

'I that have held a land between twin lips
And turned large England to a little kiss . . .
Yea, I am found the woman in all tales,
The face caught always in the story's face;
I, Helen, holding Paris by the lips,
Smote Hector through the head; I, Cressida,
So kissed men's mouths that they went sick and mad.'

But on the advent of Queen Eleanor with her poisoned draught, the pride of Rosamund falls very low.

There are pleasant touches of description of the gardens of Rosamund's Bower.

> ' Hark, the rain begins,
> Slips like a bird that feels among shut leaves ;
> One—two ; it catches in the rose-branches
> Like a bird caught.
>
> . . . . . .
>
> I never loved white roses much ; but see
> How the wind drenches the low lime-branches
> With shaken silver in the rainiest leaves.'

The displaced accent of the word 'branches' in each quotation may be due to the influence of Rossetti, to whom the book is dedicated. *Rosamund* is scarcely a maturer work than *The Queen - Mother*, and yet it is to be hoped that the little book will, ere long, be reprinted. Its principal interest, no doubt, arises from the fact of its authorship, but neither play affords any reason for their author to be ashamed of his youthful handiwork.

Four years elapsed between the publica-

Dead Love, 1864. tion of these plays and of a little prose story which saw the light in 1864, called *Dead Love*. The story, told in quaint English, is of a French lady named Madame Yolande, who fell in love with the slain body of a French gentleman, Messire Jacques d'Aspremont. Possibly only a few copies of the tale were printed, for it is now of extreme rarity.

It was in the following year, 1865, that the poet produced his first masterpiece.

THE POEMS

THE POEMS

WITH the publication of *Atalanta in Calydon*
Swinburne wrote his name at once
among the great poets of the world.
The book was hailed rapturously
and immediately as a triumph of poetry.
So much indeed was written of the book at
the time of its publication, and has been
written during the subsequent years, that it
would be difficult to find anything new to
say on the subject. With the possible
exception of the first series of *Poems and
Ballads*, this play is the best known of
Swinburne's many volumes. The novelty
of its form, the originality and dexterity of
its lyrical metres, the freshness and vigour
of the blank verse, were unmistakably the
work of a poet, taken apart, if such a thing
is possible to the imagination, from the

*Atalanta in
Calydon,
1865.*

15

scholarly construction of the tragedy and
the verbal expression of sensation or emotion. From the exquisite picture of a
springtide dawn, with which the play commences, to the almost intolerable pity of
its close, there is no faltering of idea, no
cloudiness of purpose.

The prologue, placed in the mouth of
the Chief Huntsman, avoids the Euripidean
mistake of telling too much, and merely
posts the action up to the date of the
drama, with a hint of the purpose of the
fatal day to follow.

' O fair-faced sun, killing the stars and dews
  And dreams and desolation of the night,
  Rise up, shine, stretch thine hand out, with thy bow
  Touch the most dimmest height of trembling heaven,
  And burn and break the dark about thy ways,
  Shot through and through with arrows ; let thine hair
  Lighten as flame above that flameless shell
  Which was the moon, and thine eyes fill the world
  And thy lips kindle with swift beams ; let earth
  Laugh and the long sea fiery from thy feet . . .
  And all the winds about thee with their wings,
  And fountain-heads of all the watered world ;
  Each horn of Achelous and the green
  Euenus, wedded with the straitening sea.'

The chorus which follows the prologue,
taking up in a lighter lyrical strain the
theme of awakening spring, has been quoted
so often that if it were possible to refrain
from quotation here it would seem wiser
to do so. But to refrain is impossible—at
least from the quotation of three of the
seven perfect stanzas of this chorus.

' When the hounds of spring are on winter's traces,
   The mother of months in meadow or plain
Fills the shadows and windy places
   With lisp of leaves and ripple of rain ;
And the brown bright nightingale amorous
Is half assuaged for Itylus,
For the Thracian ships and the foreign faces,
   The tongueless vigil and all the pain. . . .

For winter's rains and ruins are over,
   And all the season of snows and sins ;
The days dividing lover and lover,
   The light that loses, the night that wins ;
And time remembered is grief forgotten,
And frosts are slain and flowers begotten,
And in green underwood and cover
   Blossom by blossom the spring begins.

The full streams feed on flower of rushes,
   Ripe grasses trammel a travelling foot,
The faint fresh flame of the young year flushes
   From leaf to flower and flower to fruit,

And fruit and leaf are as gold and fire,
And the oat is heard above the lyre,
And the hoofèd heel of a Satyr crushes
The chestnut-husk at the chestnut-root.'

The entrance of Althaea brings with it
the first suggestion of tragedy, breaking
harshly with the bitterness of maternal
jealousy upon the enchanting song of
spring, and with her narration of her dream
of the fire-brand, the story of the drama
begins to be unveiled. The love of the
mother for her son Meleager is so ex-
quisitely portrayed by Swinburne that it
is curious to note that his play must have
been written at the same time as the poems
of another kind of love, which aroused the
fierce indignation of the English press a
year later. Thus speaks Althaea to her
son :—

' I have seen thee all thy years
A man in arms, strong and a joy to men
Seeing thy head glitter and thine hand burn its way
Through a heavy and iron furrow of sundering spears ;
But always also a flower of three suns old,
The small one thing that lying drew down my life
To lie with thee and feed thee ; a child and weak,
Mine, a delight to no man, sweet to me.

Who then sought to thee? Who gat help? Who knew
If thou wert goodly? Nay, no man at all . . .
But fair to me thou wert, O little life,
Fruitless, the fruit of mine own flesh, and blind,
More than much gold, ungrown, a foolish flower.'

The maternal love of Althaea, the self-dedi-
cation of Atalanta to perpetual virginity,
the roughness and coarseness of Toxeus
and Plexippus are equally clearly delineated
by the dramatist.

The descriptive passage of the death of
the boar is a brilliant conquest of tremendous
difficulty. But what difficulty could there
be for a poet capable of such phrases as
these?—

'Seeing where the green ooze of a sun-struck marsh
  Shook with a thousand reeds untunable,
  And in their moist and multitudinous flower
  Slept no soft sleep, with violent visions fed,
  The blind bulk of the immeasurable beast.
  .   .   .   .

  But the boar heaved half out of ooze and slime
  His tense flank trembling round the barbèd wound,
  Hateful; and fiery with invasive eyes
  And bristling with intolerable hair
  Plunged, and the hounds clung, and green flowers and
      white
  Reddened and broke all round them where they came.
  .   .   .   .

Sprang straight and roaring with no lesser cry
Than thunder and the roar of wintering streams
That mix their own foam with the yellower sea;
And as a tower that falls by fire in fight . . .
So through crushed branches and the reddening brake
Clamoured and clashed the fervour of his feet.'

  .   .   .   .

The account of the death of the scourge
sent by Artemis is followed quickly by the
news of the slaughter of Toxeus and Plexippus by Meleager in return for an insult to
Atalanta; and Althaea goes from the stage
to throw into the fire the brand upon whose
safety depends the life of her son. Divided
between her love for her brethren and her
son, she has no hesitation and no regret.

'Girls, one thing will I say and hold my peace.
I that did this will weep not nor cry out. . . .
                 I know not if I live,
Save that I feel the fire upon my face
And on my cheek the burning of a brand.'

It was doubtless in self-oblivion that Swinburne, when writing of Tennyson's *Rizpah*,
spoke of 'the deep truth that great poets
are bi-sexual.' 'The emotion produced'
on Swinburne 'by the first reading of

Tennyson's *Rizpah* * may seem to colder readers somewhat too emotional, but the words which he uses in that wonderful essay are alone worthy of the great passage written by himself, placed in the mouth of Althaea, here, as her thoughts turn from the vision of the expiring brand to the picture of her son dying out of her sight.

> 'Yet, O child,
> Son, first-born, fairest—O sweet mouth, sweet eyes,
> That drew my life out through my suckling breast,
> That shone and clove my heart through—O soft knees
> Clinging, O tender treadings of soft feet,
> Cheeks warm with little kissings—O child, child,
> What have we made each other?   Lo, I felt
> Thy weight cleave to me, a burden of beauty, O son,
> Thy cradled brows and loveliest loving lips,
> The floral hair, the little lightening eyes,
> And all thy goodly glory ; with mine hands
> Delicately I fed thee, with my tongue
> Tenderly spake, saying, Verily, in God's time,
> For all the little likeness of thy limbs,
> Son, I shall make thee a kingly man to fight,
> A lordly leader ; and hear before I die,
> "She bore the goodliest sword of all the world." '

The return of the hunters, 'the feast turned

---

* 'Tennyson and Musset,' in *Miscellanies*.

funeral' is set to a grave lyrical music, like a funeral march, as noble as Beethoven.

> ' Let your hands meet
>   Round the weight of my head ;
> Lift ye my feet
>   As the feet of the dead ;
> For the flesh of my body is molten, the limbs of it molten
>   as lead.'

Henceforward to the end the drama is solemn and pure pathos. The long and stately farewell speech of Meleager—less passionate and agonised than that of Othello, but similar in its recollection of past triumphs—is but spoilt by quotation, and yet I cannot leave the play without a transcription of a few lines, the last words of the dying man to Atalanta.

> ' But thou, dear, touch me with thy rose-like hands,
>   And fasten up mine eyelids with thy mouth,
>   A bitter kiss ; and grasp me with thine arms,
>   Printing with heavy lips my light waste flesh,
>   Made light and thin by heavy-handed fate ;
>   And with thy holy maiden eyes drop dew,
>   Drop tears for dew upon me who am dead,
>   Me who have loved thee ; seeing without sin done
>   I am gone down to the empty weary house

Where no flesh is, nor beauty nor swift eyes,
Nor sound of mouth nor might of hands and feet.

. . . . . .

And now for God's sake kiss me once and twice
And let me go ; for the night gathers me,
And in the night shall no man gather fruit.'

To pour out upon the shrine of this tragedy an hyperbole of praise would be but waste labour. The 'very flower and crown' of the work of a great poet stands above the need of praise; and I doubt whether any critic will ever dispute the supremacy of *Atalanta* over the rest of the poems of this poet, for nobility, for pathos, for command of language, for beauty, for all that goes to the making of poetry. The development of lyrical metre in the later works perhaps gives to the restrained use of metre in these choruses a sense of immaturity—a sense wholly fictitious, be it said—which otherwise they would not have possessed. Yet perhaps one would give all the choruses of *Erectheus* for these. The nobility, the solemn beauty of the blank verse have never been surpassed by its author. The indescribable flavour or savour which tells one at once whether a piece of writing is of the highest kind or not is present in *Atalanta* as it is absent from much of his later work. Such a poem as *Atalanta* is an admirable example of the trite saying that a poet is born, not made. It was published by its author at the age of twenty-eight; but twenty or thirty years of study and practice of literature since then have not given to the poet a surer hand, a sweeter note or a swifter imagination. It is a piece of inspiration, above and beyond the world of mere literary craftmanship. The last eighteen pages are as musical as Shelley, as noble as Sophocles, as pathetic as Shakespeare.

Though later published, the dramatic poem of *Chastelard* is generally understood to be an earlier written work than that of *Atalanta*, but to have been subjected to a subsequent revision. This, the first of the three plays which

Chastelard, 1865.

Swinburne has devoted to Mary Stuart, is little more than an episode in the career of that exceptional woman. If the tempestuous nature of the greater part of Swinburne's work may ever have tempted any unwise critic to regard the poet as a creature of spasmodic influences, the continuity of purpose manifested in these three plays, published over a period of sixteen years, is a definite answer to so foolish a complaint. To any poet not endowed with a vast capacity for research, assimilation of matter and patient labour, the writing of such three plays as *Chastelard*, *Bothwell*, and *Mary Stuart* would have been an impossibility. Even the 'gentle Shakespeare' one can hardly imagine capable of the long and heavy labour necessary for the writing of the enormous volume of *Bothwell*, which, nevertheless, has been endured by a poet of a very much less equable temperament. The notes in prose which Swinburne has appended to his plays in later volumes of criticism,* are obvious evidence of his prac-

* Vide *Miscellanies*.

tical devotion to the earthlier or more prosaic details of his poems. It is clear from these that even if such a historian as Mr Lecky has no conception of what poetry should be, at all events in such a poet as Swinburne there was lost a very brilliant and practical historian.

In *Chastelard* there is a foretaste of the even more 'violent delights' of the first series of *Poems and Ballads*. Here, for the first time, we hear that acknowledgment of love as a blind, venomous, senseless and overmastering insanity, which is the *leit-motif* of Swinburne's love poems. With Swinburne, love is barely a human passion. With Catullus, to whom he comes nearest— if we exclude Sappho, known alas! but in fragments—love is human enough; the desire of body for body, the lust of exclusive possession, the rut of a strong animal, softened and tempered with laughter and tenderness. With other poets, love tends much farther towards sentiment, the more usual emotions. But the desire of Swinburne's lovers is almost a disembodied flame,

a thing which the possession of neither soul
nor body could satisfy. In the greater part
of his work there is less human emotion than
there is in many a little poem of Browning's.
Such keener pity as the romance of Chastelard might beget in us if touched by a
tenderer hand, Swinburne throws aside. A
curious note in this tragedy—the force of
which appears in the later play of *Mary
Stuart*—is that, while its readers are left
unmoved by the death of the principal actor
in it, so far as he himself is concerned, their
pity is called on by the suffering of a minor
character. We sympathise not with Chastelard—who asks for no sympathy—but with
Mary Beaton. The strength of Chastelard,
devoured as he is by a love which he
knows to be insane and yet cannot
escape from, is wholly admirable. Chastelard, moreover, is an epicure of emotion—
an artist in sensation. He cultivates his
insanity, knowing it to be for him the only
thing worth life and death. It is with
contempt only that he thinks of Darnley,
who, he says,—

> 'Shall have
> This fare for common days'-bread, which to me
> Should be a touch kept always on my sense
> To make hell soft, yea, the keen pain of hell
> Soft as the loosening of wound arms in sleep.'

Again, in his last scene with Mary, he says,—

> 'I am right glad
> That I must never feel a bitterer thing
> Than your soft curled-up shoulder and amorous arms
> From this time forth; nothing can hap to me
> Less good than this for all my whole life through.
> I would not have some new pain after this
> Come spoil the savour.'

Like the lover of Lesbia, Chastelard is not blind to the faults of his mistress. 'Did I not know you to the bone, my sweet?' he cries, in the last scene with his mistress in which after having sent him his reprieve she comes to reclaim it. To Mary Beaton at an earlier date he has said,—

> 'I know her ways of loving, all of them:
> A sweet soft way the first is; afterward
> It burns and bites like fire; the end of that,
> Charred dust and eyelids bitten through with smoke.'

Yet even his devotion to that 'sweet

serpent' of France and Scotland has one
moment of bitterness, when, after 'the most
sweet talk men ever heard of,' Mary an-
nounces to the lords who break in upon the
enchanted hour her intended marriage to
Darnley.

> ' I was just thinking how such things were made
> And were so fair as this is.'

Historical comment upon these three plays
must be left reluctantly to those who possess
a wider knowledge of the subject or have
leisure to acquire it. But it is clear that in
this play of *Chastelard*, Swinburne has built
up from the most meagre of hints an edifice
of imagination as imposing—relatively—as
those raised by Shakespeare on the sketchy
foundation of Italian novelettes. The only
two 'conscious violations of historical chron-
ology' are confessed by the writer himself in
his ' Note on the Character of Mary Queen of
Scots ' : one only is of a little importance in
a poetic view of the play, the other of none.

The play is essentially the work of a
young man. Writing in late years, its
author speaks somewhat contemptuously of

'the suicidal young monomaniac' upon whom he had lavished so much care and sympathy in the past. The prodigality and quality of the emotion poured out upon such a theme as that of *Chastelard* by a young poet are essentially alien to the increased calm of years. The theme of hopeless love was then the keynote of the utterances of the author of *Poems and Ballads*. But the restraint of himself, the even greater care expended upon the character of Mary than on that of the lover of whom she was tired, are remarkable.

Her cautious diplomacy in the attempt to rid herself of her lover, her sudden jealousy for the moment dispelling her weariness or her prudence, her anxiety lest he might not be killed before he could tarnish her reputation—such as it was!—the constant changes of her mood between this anxiety and her passing emotional regrets, and finally her utter faithlessness and callousness; all these phases in the temperament of the vicious and fascinating woman are admirably delineated by a dramatist perfectly conscious of his aim. With the portrayal of the character of Chastelard the dramatist had a somewhat simpler task. The soldier-poet is, however, an admirable creation. His determination to die by the command of his mistress, 'in royal purple fashion,' his gentleness to her in spite of his knowledge of her vicious selfishness, his loyalty to her fame—these characteristics render him an actor worthy of admiration and sympathy; while the beauty of the words placed in his mouth are apt as coming from the mouth of a poet. For choice of quotation the beauty of his soliloquy at the beginning of the prison scene is preferable.

' So here my time shuts up; and the last light
  Has made the last shade in the world for me.
  The sunbeam that was narrow like a leaf
  Has turned a hand and the hand stretched to an arm,
  And the arm has reached the dust on the floor, and made
  A maze of motes with paddling fingers. Well,
  I knew not that a man so sure to die
  Could care so little; a bride-night's lustiness
  Leaps in my veins as light fire under a wind.

  Ah, in my weary dusty space of sight
  Her face will float with heavy scents of hair

And fire of subtle, amorous eyes, and lips
More hot than wine, full of sweet wicked words
Babbled against mine own lips, and long hands
Spread out and pale bright throat and pale bright
       breasts,
Fit to make all men mad.   I do believe
This fire shall never quite burn out to the ash
And leave no heat and flame upon my dust
For witness where a man's heart was burned up.
For all Christ's work this Venus is not quelled,
But reddens at the mouth with blood of men,
Sucking between small teeth the sap o' the veins,
Dabbling with death her little tender lips—
A bitter beauty, poisonous pearlèd mouth.
I am not fit to live but for love's sake,
So I were best die shortly.   Ah, fair love,
Fair fearful Venus made of deadly foam,
I shall escape you somehow with my death—
Your splendid supple body and mouth on fire
And Paphian breath that bites the lips with heat . . .'

The passionate beauty of the whole scene
when the queen comes to reclaim the reprieve she has sent, and which he has
already destroyed, is superb.   What love has
ever gone much farther than that implied in
these words he addresses to her, words that
are also the bitterest of indictments?—

  ' Why should one woman have all goodly things?
    You have all beauty ; let mean women's lips

Be pitiful and speak truth : they will not be
Such perfect things as yours.   Be not ashamed
That hands not made like these that snare men's souls
Should do men good, give alms, relieve men's pain ;
You have the better, being more fair than they,
They are half foul, being rather good than fair ;
You are quite fair ; to be quite fair is best.'

But if any further proof were needed of
the dramatic genius of the author of this
play, it is supplied a little further on by a
few lines of which only a poet of the highest
and finest imagination could be capable.
They make the most tragic point in the
whole tragedy, and I remember nothing
quite like them in dramatic literature for
horror of premonition, for irony, for the
suggestion of tragedy deeper than the actual
one on the stage.   The queen has said.—

'I am sure

I shall die somehow sadly.'

He replies :—

'. . . You, die like me ?

Stretch your throat out that I may kiss all round
Where mine shall be cut through : suppose my mouth
The axe-edge to bite so sweet a throat in twain
With bitter iron, should not it turn soft
As lip is soft to lip ? '

C

The final touch of tragic suggestion, after the execution of Chastelard witnessed from a window in Holyrood by Mary Carmichael and Mary Beaton, is supplied by the last two lines of the play. The infamy of Mary Stuart is suggested by the words of Mary Carmichael describing the scene to Mary Beaton, who sits away from the window.

> 'She bends and laughs a little, graciously,
> And turns half, talking to I know not whom—
> A big man with great shoulders ; ah, the face,
> You get his face now—wide and duskish, yea,
> The youth burned out of it.   A goodly man,
> Thewed mightily and sunburned to the bone.'

Then after the execution is over, the two women are disturbed by an usher.

> ' Make way there for the Lord of Bothwell, room—
> Place for my Lord of Bothwell next the queen.'

And this is the end of Chastelard.

It is a common mistake of later critics to underrate the value of this play. That it is extremely beautiful and admirably constructed goes for nothing in the eyes of such a one as he whose sketch of the poet's work lies before me now. ' Deservedly less successful ' than *Atalanta* is his sole criticism of *Chastelard*. The two plays cannot in strictness be compared with each other. The dramatic treatment of each is as different as the subject. The poet of *Atalanta* had a subject which allowed him a freer scope for the display of metrical power than the poet of *Chastelard*. The brilliant notation of Mary's successive changes of intention or mood is more elaborate even than Shakespeare's rendering of the fleeting moods of Cleopatra. It is an admirable play and a beautiful poem, and as such it could have been written by no man who had not at once dramatic and poetic genius ; as to what it is itself, it could not have been written by any man but Swinburne. In my own view, the place of *Chastelard* is among the finest, not among the least fine, of the poet's works.

For the majority of readers of poetry the name and fame of Swinburne are in-

Poems and Ballads. First Series, 1866.

separably and eternally connected with the first volume of lyrical poems published by him. It is possible, though it is not—thank Heaven!—probable, that such a play as *Chastelard* might have been forgotten, such a poem as *Atalanta* lost sight of, in the whirl of past and new books, if their author had not been permitted to supplement them. But it was with the publication of the first series of *Poems and Ballads* that he made himself an eternal place in the literature of the world. There was no question thenceforward possible as to the quality of the poet's capacity. Such a volume was absolutely unparalleled in the world's history, for originality and variety of metre, for fulness of utterance, for music, for volubility of erotic passion. It is a volume which, of course, must shine with a more brilliant light upon the years of youth than in the days when the hey-day in the blood of the imagination is tame

and humble. I can compare the effect of
the first reading of this volume upon myself,
a dozen years ago, to nothing but the re-
velation of a new world.

> ' Then felt I like some watcher of the skies
> When a new planet swims into his ken.'

The effect of the miraculous novelty and
diversity of the metres, the astounding feats
of rhythm and rhyme upon a boy for the
first time struggling to express himself in
verse, the vehement and absolute expression of emotions and sensations half felt and
wholly thirsted after, has had no parallel in
my recollections of books or things.

But when the first charm of these poems
has vanished, when the delighted shock of
that earliest rapture has passed away, when
one's heart no longer aches with the magnificent sorrow of the poem named *The
Triumph of Time*, or maddens to the
sanguine rhythms of *Dolores*, there is much
that remains for a perennial delight. And
yet it is a volume which could only be
applauded worthily by a writer not much

over twenty, since it is to the very young
that it appeals most.   After twenty, one
has other things to think of than—

'The laurel, the palms and the pæan, the breast of the
    nymphs in the brake ;
  Breasts more soft than a dove's, that tremble with tenderer
    breath ;
  And all the wings of the loves, and all the joy before
    death.'

One has fallen from that high state of
Hedonism ; 'the world is too much with
us'; and our enjoyment of the poems—
which must be known by heart for full
appreciation—is often an enjoyment of the
memory of an earlier delight.   But what
an amazing book it is!   The volcanic
exuberance of its metres and rhymes is
not more astounding than its sustained
ebullience of amorous imagination, its
metrical music and beautiful verbiage
than its frenzied erotomania.

The book, indeed, is a product of artistic
mania rather than of human impulse.   The
most violent of its poems are, as it were,
the visions of an opium eater, the dreams

of an exasperated imagination. They are 'of imagination all compact'; spiritual rather than fleshly. Their passion is for nothing realisable or tangible: their loves are the loves of a Faust in his study brooding over fancied deliria of beauty and lust and blood. Even the satiety of which some of the poems speak has nothing human about it. The poet has aimed not at the expression of ordinary emotions, but at the expression of superhuman frenzy, inexhaustible suffering and delight.

The volume opens with two ballads in the Italian manner, which Rossetti made more familiar by his later-published translations. The following poem, entitled *Laus Veneris*, is a monologue placed in the mouth of Tannhäuser after his return to the Horselberg from his unsuccessful pilgrimage. It is at this point, where the story is usually made to end, that, in Swinburne's eyes, the tragedy begins. In Wagner's music-poem, Tannhäuser dies on his return from Rome: a deviation from the legend. In this poem the tragedy lies

in the return of the man who believes in
Christ to the diabolic goddess, 'that thing
transformed that was the Cytherean,' in
his craving for Christ and damnation to
Venus. The chief triumph of the poem is
its splendid conquest of the simple, un-
ideaed medieval spirit. It might have been
written by a superstitious monk, firmly con-
vinced that an evil goddess lurked in the
hollow mountain.

> ' Inside the Horsel here the air is hot ;
>   Right little peace one hath for it, God wot ;
>   The scenty, dusted daylight burns the air,
>   And my heart chokes me till I hear it not.'

The symbolism of Wagner is absent here.
Venus is no abstraction, but an incarna-
tion. Tannhäuser speaks thus :—

> ' So that one dawn I rode forth sorrowing ;
>   I had no hope but of some evil thing,
>   And so rode slowly past the windy wheat,
>   And past the vineyard and the water-spring,
>
>   Up to the Horsel. A great elder-tree
>   Held back its heaps of flowers to let me see
>   The ripe tall grass, and one that walked therein
>   Naked, with hair shed over to the knee.'

The idea of the multitudinous devilries

and evil delights of the subterranean palace
which fills the 'Venusberg Music' is absent
in this simpler conception. The weariness
of Tannhäuser is of the hot air, the scent
and shadow, the insatiable lips 'curled like
a tiger's that curl back to feed,' the clinging body; and he longs for the place
where—

> 'Blue ripples blow,
>
> The blue curled eddies of the blowing Rhine,
> I felt the sharp wind shaking grass and vine
>   Touch my blood too, and sting me with delight
> Through all this waste and weary body of mine
>
> That never feels clear air . . .'

He craves for a respite from over-much
pleasure, the beds that are 'full of perfume
and sad sound,' the halls that 'drip with
flower-like red.'

> 'Ah, yet would God this flesh of mine might be
> Where air might wash and long leaves cover me,
>   Where tides of grass break into foam of flowers,
> Or where the wind's feet shine along the sea.'

The archaic style of the *Laus Veneris* is
probably due to the influence of William
Morris. The manner of the beautiful poem

called *The Triumph of Time* seems to me
somewhat after the fashion of Browning, but
the writer himself, it is understood, attributes
its sentiment to Byron.   This is, I think,
unjust to himself.   One may despair and
suffer remorse without necessarily donning
the mantle of Childe Harold.   However that
may be, the poem is even farther beyond the
capacity of Byron than of Browning.   In it
the writer has indeed given voice, though he
declares it to be impossible, to—

> 'The word that a man might say
> Whose whole life's love goes down in a day.'

The poem opens with a hint of a despair
which is too great for utterance, but the
regret for all that is lost breaks soon into
words.

> 'In the change of years, in the coil of things,
>   In the clamour and rumour of life to be,
> We drinking love at the furthest springs,
>   Covered with love as a covering tree,
> We had grown as gods, as the gods above,
> Filled from the heart to the lips with love,
> Held fast in his hands, clothed warm with his wings,
>   O love, my love, had you loved but me!'

The aching eyes fall on the low downs

leaning to the sea, where 'the strong sea-daisies feast on the sun,' and in the sea the speaker finds the images of his regret, in the waifs washed up and left by the ebb-tide,

> ' Weed from the water, grass from a grave,
>   A broken blossom, a ruined rhyme.'

Then the bitterness of thwarted possession finds voice.

> ' I wish we were dead together to-day,
>   Lost sight of, hidden away out of sight,
> Clasped and clothed in the cloven clay,
>   Out of the world's way, out of the light,
> Out of the ages of worldly weather,
> Forgotten of all men altogether,
> As to the world's first dead, taken wholly away,
>   Made one with death, filled full of the night.'

The thought of suicide,

> ' I will go down to the great sweet mother,
>   Mother and lover of men, the sea,'

turns to the knowledge of the evanescence of grief, and after the narration of the episode of that singer 'who lived in France of old' and died as his mistress laid her lips to his— 'O brother, the gods were good to you,' he cries—the poem ends with the intention of resignation to life, with a closing thought of eternal separation.

> ' I shall never tell you on earth; and in heaven,
>   If I cry to you then, will you hear or know? '

The fragment in imitation of a Greek play dealing with the love of Phædra for Hippolytus, the poems labelled *Les Noyades*, *A Leave-Taking* and *Satia Te Sanguine*, are written on the same subject of a hopeless love. The lyric of *Itylus* is one of the poet's most perfect poems.

> ' Swallow, my sister, O sister swallow,
>   How can thine heart be full of the spring?
>   A thousand summers are over and dead.
> What hast thou found in the spring to follow?
> What hast thou found in thy heart to sing?
>   What wilt thou do when the summer is shed? '

The verses entitled *Anactoria* grew out of an attempt to render into English the words of Sappho, but the task proving insuperable, the poet set himself the more profitable labour of writing a poem which should include the spirit of Sappho and here and there her actual words. It is, of course, known to most readers that one of the two

of Sappho's poems which have come down
to us complete is generally styled—though
not so named by the poetess herself—the
Ode to Anactoria. The strange, insatiable
cruelty of love expressed in Swinburne's
poem is, however, due to Swinburne rather
than to the Lesbian singer. The poem is
to me a little hard and cold, though as a
matter of verse-writing it ranks among the
poet's finest pieces. The triumph in the
knowledge of her immortality, placed in the
mouth of Sappho, lifts the conclusion of the
poem above the sensual savagery of its
beginning.

' Yea, thou shalt be forgotten like spilt wine,
   Except these kisses of my lips on thine
   Brand them with immortality ; but me . . .
   . . . Of me the high God hath not all His will.
   Blossom of branches and on each high hill
   Clear air and wind, and under in clamorous vales
   Fierce noises of the fiery nightingales,
   Buds burning in the sudden spring like fire,
   The wan washed sand and the wave's vain desire,
   Sails seen like blown white flowers at sea, and words
   That bring tears swiftest, and long notes of birds
   Violently singing till the whole world sings—
   I, Sappho, shall be one with all these things,
   With all high things forever.'

The *Hymn to Proserpine*, 'after the proclamation in Rome of the Christian Faith,' placed in the mouth of a regretful pagan, is one of the most widely known of Swinburne's poems, as much for its religious antipathies as its music. One of its most famous passages is the comparison between the mother of the Galilean and the mother of Eros.

' For thine came pale and a maiden and sister to
    sorrow ; but ours,
Her deep hair heavily laden with odour and colour of
    flowers . . .
For thine came weeping, a slave among slaves, and
    rejected ; but she
Came flushed from the full-flushed wave, and imperial,
    her foot on the sea.'

And another :—

' Will ye bridle the deep sea with chains, will ye chasten
    the high sea with rods ?
Will ye take her to chain her with chains, who is older
    than all ye gods ?
All ye as a wind shall go by, as a fire shall ye pass and
    be past ;
Ye are gods and behold, ye shall die and the waves
    be upon you at last.

In the darkness of time, in the deeps of the years, in
    the changes of things,
Ye shall sleep as a slain man sleeps and the world
    shall forget you for kings.'

Pagan again is the contemplation of death
in the poem called *Ilicet*.

  ' There is an end of joy and sorrow ;
    Peace all day long, all night, all morrow,
      But never a time to laugh or weep.
    The end is come of pleasant places,
    The end of tender words and faces,
      The end of all, the poppied sleep . . .

  A little sorrow, a little pleasure
    Fate metes us from the dusty measure
      That holds the date of all of us ;
    We are born with travail and strong crying,
    And from the birth-day to the dying
      The likeness of our life is thus.'

There is, it need scarcely be said, no
touch of impure thought in the four perfect
sonnets to the statue in the Louvre of the
Hermaphroditus, the delicate Greek conception of the sexless being of two sexes.

  ' Love stands upon thy left hand and thy right,
    Yet by no sunset and by no moonrise
    Shall make thee man and ease a woman's sighs
  Or make thee woman for a man's delight.'

I have no time here to touch upon many a little poem exhibiting some curious feature of thought or invention of metre and rhyme.

The *Faustine* is a singular *tour de force*, each of its forty-one stanzas containing a rhyme to Faustine.

> 'You could do all things but be good
>   Or chaste of mien ;
> And that you would not if you could,
>   We know, Faustine.'

The origin of this poem has been told us by the writer in his 'Notes on Poems and Reviews'—the sudden sight of a face in a crowd which recalled the image of the Roman Faustina. The *Leper* is a strange and terrible little poem, born from an old French story. For the famous poem *Dolores*, apart from its astonishing metrical achievement, I have no great love. The rush and the rhythm of it are, of course, superb, but there is little depth below its troubled surface. The metrical ingenuity of it is beyond all praise and conception. It can perhaps be best appreciated by placing beside it a verse of Byron's in the same measure, which may be, however, condemned to small type in a footnote.*

It was such intolerable doggerel as this which Swinburne found to his hand, and he turned it into such verse as follows. The picture is of the Roman gladiatorial circus.

> ' On sands by the storm never shaken
>   Nor wet from the washing of tides ;
> Nor by foam of the waves overtaken
>   Nor winds that the thunder bestrides ;
> But red from the print of thy paces,
>   Made smooth for the world and its lords,
> Ringed round with a flame of fair faces
>   And splendid with swords. . . .
>
> When with flame all around him aspirant,
>   Stood flushed, as a harp-player stands,
> The implacable, beautiful tyrant,
>   Rose-crowned, having death in his hands ;
> And a sound as the sound of loud water
>   Smote far through the flight of the fires,
> And mixed with the lightning of slaughter
>   A thunder of lyres.'

---

* ' Though the day of my destiny's over,
    And the star of my fate hath declined,
 Thy soft heart refused to discover
    The faults which so many could find ;
 Though thy soul with my grief was acquainted,
    It shrunk not to share it with me,
 And the love which my spirit hath painted
    It never hath found but in thee.'

The meaning and images of the poem are somewhat unusual to English ears, and certain of its phrases no doubt went far towards raising the storm which followed the publication of the book. Among the best known is the antithesis of the 'lilies and languors of virtue' and the 'raptures and roses of vice,' an antithesis full no doubt of juvenile enthusiasm, but not a principle to be taken very seriously.

The riot of *Dolores* is followed by the peace of *The Garden of Proserpine* and the dactylic verses of *Hesperia*, which possess a gracious charm for remembrance, the quiet divinity of a sunset.

'Out of the golden, remote wild west where the sea
      without shore is,
         Full of the sunset, and sad, if at all, with the fulness
            of joy,
      As a wind sets in with the autumn that blows from the
            region of stories,
         Blows with a perfume of songs and of memories be-
            loved from a boy,

.   .   .   .

From the bountiful, infinite west, from the happy
      memorial places
         Full of the stately repose and the lordly delight of the
            dead

> Where the fortunate islands are lit with the light of
> ineffable faces,
> And the sound of a sea without wind is about them
> and sunset is red.'

The quieter tones of the book are not among its least acceptable utterances. Of such are the quiet, regretful lines *In Memory of Walter Savage Landor*, or the cool fragrance of *The Sundew*, the little marsh-plant of the northern moors.

> 'The deep scent of the heather burns
> About it; breathless though it be,
> Bow down and worship; more than we
> Is the least flower whose life returns,
> Least weed renascent in the sea.'

The longer poem called *Félise* is perfectly delightful with its light, half-regretful mirth, its touches of natural beauty. It narrates simply the parting of two lovers, the one a little tired and careless, the other a little regretful.

Mais où sont les neiges d'antan? The poem bears as its mocking motto the refrain of Villon's *ballade*.

'What shall be said between us here
   Among the downs, between the trees,
In fields that knew our feet last year,
   In sight of quiet lands and seas,
      This year, Félise?

.   .   .   .   .   .

Here as last year the fields begin
   A fire of flowers and glowing grass;
The old fields we laughed and lingered in,
   Seeing each our souls in last year's glass,
      Félise, alas!'

But last year's leaves and flowers are
where the snows are.

'I had died for this last year, to know
   You loved me. Who shall turn on fate?
I care not if love come or go
   Now, though your love seek mine for mate.
      It is too late.'

Laughter and mockery, and yet a little
regret; weariness, and yet a little longing,
are all blended here, chasing each other
like butterflies until the very last.

'Live and let live, as I will do,
   Love and let love, and so will I.
But, sweet, for me no more with you:
   Not while I live, not though I die.
      Good-night, good-bye.'

The bright and joyous little poem which follows, *An Interlude*, has the freshness of boyhood captured only once before in the *Hero and Leander* of Marlowe, while the rhymed stories of *St Dorothy* and *The Two Dreams* match in beauty the narrative poems of Keats.

In the dedicatory verses to Burne-Jones, the poet has gone back again to the metre of *Dolores*, investing it with a fresh charm, and while bidding farewell almost regretfully to his own book, with its ' daughters of dreams and of stories,' he has summed up in two lines the most characteristic qualities of himself and the great painter.

> ' In a land of clear colours and stories,
>   In a region of shadowless hours,
>   Where earth has a garment of glories
>   And a murmur of musical flowers ;
>   In woods where the spring half uncovers
>   The flush of her amorous face,
>   By the waters that listen for lovers,
>   For these is there place ?
>
> .   .   .   .
>
>   Though the world of your hands be more gracious
>   And lovelier in lordship of things
>   Clothed round by sweet art with the spacious
>   Warm heaven of her imminent wings,

Let them enter unfledged and nigh fainting
    For the love of old loves and lost times ;
And receive in your palace of painting
    This revel of rhymes.'

The phrase is perfect.

Of the *Poems and Ballads* one feels at twenty only the fervour of emotion, the unsurpassed achievement of metrical ingenuity. A few years later, however, one finds in it a certain want of actual human interest. It is for this reason that the book should be written of by a critic not long out of his teens if it is to receive the criticism of the emotional admiration it begets in us in earlier years. The poet has played many tunes on the theme of sexual emotion save those of the more usual sentiment of love of which Amestris and Aholibah know nothing. The tunes after a time lose some of their charm, but the manner of the playing remains marvellous to the end. No poet has ever possessed such a command over lyrical metres, such a power over words, as that shown by Swinburne in his first volume of lyrical poems. The rapture of writing, the delight of involved rhyme and metre, the joy of verbal music, are visible in no other book so clearly as in this. As it is the most startling and strange of its author's many volumes, so it will probably be to the end of time the best known.

The contrast between the first series of
Songs before Sunrise, 1871. *Poems and Ballads* and the volume which followed it in order of publication is peculiarly sharp. The sudden transition from the hothouse atmosphere of erotic emotions to the keen air of the mountain-peaks and wild waste places of the *Songs before Sunrise* is something more than surprising. The *Songs before Sunrise* are mystic, prophetic, ascetic, spiritual, even at times arid. The same passion of soul breathes through each book, but the object of the passion is changed. It is no longer the desire for the tangible or intangible bodies of women, but the spiritual if no less stormy desire for all that is denoted by the word Freedom.

The purport of the book is twofold. On
the one hand it is an accompaniment to the
Italian revolution which inspired it : on the
other it is a more universal, less ephemeral,
celebration of the same spirit of Liberty
which drew the adoration of Shelley. It is
a mistake to consider literally the political
sentiments of the volume. The book is
essentially visionary and mystic. The
thought that the voice of Italy should at
any time

> ' Awake from her tomb
> England, and France from her prison,
> Sisters, a star by a star '

would from a practical point of view be just
cause for a month's laughter, while in the
light of later suns the 'strident, anti-Gallican
cackle' of Tennyson—

> ' God bless the narrow sea which keeps her off,'

is more acceptable than Swinburne's blan-
dishments when the enthusiasm of his
early years instructs us in the sisterhood of
England and France. But the political or
international views of the volume call for

wider criticism than this, and are not based upon contemporary quarrels.

The volume is dedicated to Mazzini. Its prelude is an attempt to reconcile whatever discrepancy there may appear to be between the book and its forerunner.

> ' Between the green bud and the red
>   Youth sat and sang by time, and shed
>   From eyes and tresses flowers and tears,
>   From heart and spirit hopes and fears,
>   Upon the hollow stream whose bed
>   Is channelled by the foamless years ;
>   And with the white the gold-haired head
>   Mixed running locks and in Time's ears
>   Youth's dreams hung singing, and Time's truth
>   Was half not harsh in the ears of youth.'

And, learning wisdom, youth

> ' Felt the winds round him shake and shower
>   The rose-red and the blood-red leaf,
>   Delight whose germ grew never grain
>   And passion dyed in its own pain.'

And the poet himself speaks thus :—

> ' We too have tracked by star-proof trees
>   The tempest of the Thyiades
>   Scare the loud night on hills that hid
>   The blood-feasts of the Bassarid,

> Heard their song's iron cadences
>   Fright the wolf hungering from the kid,
> Outroar the lion-throated seas,
>   Outchide the north wind if it chid,
> And hush the torrent-tongued ravines
> With thunders of their tambourines.'

But the flutes and drums and tongues of fire that 'called on Cotys by her name Edonian' are silent, and only the 'ageless rhyme' of the stars and the light of the soul remain, undefeated by passions and pleasures, undestroyed by time and change.

The *Eve of Revolution*, which follows the prelude, is a tremendous poem in the spirit of the *Odes to Liberty* and *To Naples*, but in the language and allegorical manner of Isaiah rather than of Shelley. I transcribe one stanza out of twenty-seven.

> ' Light, light and light ! to break and melt in sunder
>   All clouds and chains that in one bondage bind
> Eyes, hands and spirits, forged by fear and wonder
>   And sleek, fierce fraud with hidden knife behind ;
> There goes no fire from heaven before their thunder,
>   Nor are the links not malleable that wind
> Round the snared limbs and souls that ache there-
>   under ;
>   The hands are mighty, were the head not blind.

Priest is the staff of king
And chains and cloud one thing,
And fettered flesh with devastated mind.
Open thy soul to see,
Slave, and thy feet are free;
Thy bonds and thy beliefs are one in kind,
And of thy fears thine irons wrought
Hang weights upon thee fashioned out of thine own
thought.'

There seem to be several classes into which the poems of this volume may be divided: the mystic, such as *Hertha*, *Genesis* and *The Hymn of Man;* the imaginative or pictorial, such as *Mater Triumphalis*, *The Pilgrims*, the *Eve of Revolution;* the actual, such as *The Halt before Rome*, *An Appeal* and *Siena*. The mystic poems are written round a species of pantheistic philosophy akin to, even if not founded on, the doctrine of Emerson. The poem *Hertha* is a vague paraphrase of the idea of the Oversoul.

' I am that which began;
Out of me the years roll,
Out of me God and man;
I am equal and whole;
God changes, and man, and the form of them bodily;
I am the soul.'

The *Hymn of Man,* a further development of the same idea, traces the course of the world from 'the grey beginning of years' to the outburst of life on the earth,

> 'Was it Love brake forth flower-fashion, a bird with gold on his wings?'

and to the final panegyric of a future faith,

> 'Glory to Man in the highest! for Man is the master of things.'

The verses *To Walt Whitman in America* have a sonorous rush of music unequalled in their way among all the poems of Swinburne.

> 'Send but a song oversea for us,
>   Heart of their hearts who are free,
> Heart of their singer, to be for us
>   More than our singing can be;
> Ours, in the tempest at error,
> With no light but the twilight of terror;
>   Send us a song oversea!
>
> Sweet smelling of pine-leaves and grasses,
>   And blown as a tree through and through
> With the winds of the keen mountain-passes,
>   And tender as sun-smitten dew;
> Sharp-tongued as the winter that shakes
> The wastes of your limitless lakes,
>   Wide-eyed as the sea-line's blue. . . .

.   .   .   .   .   .

Out of the sea beyond sunset,
From the evening whence morning shall be,
With the rollers in measureless onset,
With the van of the storming sea,
With the world-wide wind, with the breath
That breaks ships driven upon death,
With the passion of all things free,

With the sea-steeds footless and frantic,
White myriads for death to bestride
In the charge of the ruining Atlantic,
Where deaths by regiments ride,
With clouds and clamours of waters,
With a long note shriller than slaughter's
On the furrowless fields world-wide. . . .'

The rhythmic rush and strength and exaltation of the *Mater Triumphalis* are almost equally fine.

' Mother of man's time-travelling generations,
Breath of his nostrils, heartblood of his heart,
God above all gods worshipped of all nations,
Light above light, law beyond law, thou art.

.   .   .   .

Thou art the player whose organ-keys are thunders,
And I beneath thy foot the pedal prest ;
Thou art the ray whereat the rent night sunders,
And I the cloudlet borne upon thy breast.

I shall burn up before thee, pass and perish
As haze in sunrise on the red sea-line ;

But thou from dawn to sunsetting shalt cherish
    The thoughts that led and souls that lighted mine.
  .   .   .   .

I am thy storm thrush of the days that darken,
    Thy petrel in the foam that bears thy bark
To port through night and tempest; if thou hearken,
    My voice is in thy heaven before the lark.

My song is in the mist that hides thy morning,
    My cry is up before the day for thee ;
I have heard thee and beheld thee and give warning
    Before thy wheels divide the sky and sea. . . .'

Perhaps not even do the *Poems and Ballads* exhibit the poet's tremendous command over metres and rhythms as fully as the *Songs before Sunrise*. The writer's acquaintance with the literature of the Old Testament appears in each volume. In the poem called *Super Flumina Babylonis* he has written a species of chant for intonation round the Biblical phrase with which it commences.

' By the waters of Babylon we sat down and wept,
    Remembering thee,
That for ages of agony hast endured and slept
    And wouldst not see.'

Another Biblical phrase, ' Watchman, what

of the night?' no doubt inspired the poem
called *A Watch in the Night*. One of the
best known poems in the book is *The
Pilgrims*, written as it were round some
allegorical picture of the way-worn followers
of the Light.

'Who is your lady of love, O ye that pass
  Singing? and it is for sorrow of that which was
    That ye sing gladly or dream of what shall be?
    For gladly at once and sadly it seems ye sing.
—Our lady of love by you is unbeholden;
For hands she hath none, nor eyes, nor lips, nor golden
    Treasure of hair, nor face nor form; but we
    That love, we know her more fair than anything.'

The poem *Messidor* with its refrain,
'Put in the sickles and reap,' is inspired
with the spirit of the French Revolution,
the spirit of the uprising of the 'dumb,
dread people that sat as corpses cast in
a pit,'

    'The dumb dread people that sat
      All night without screen for the night,
      All day without food for the day.'

Tyranny and cruelty have never found
anything but an enemy in Swinburne and

for the accompanying evil of poverty he is not without sympathy. Thus in the *Litany of Nations* he writes :—

' By the sightless souls and fleshless limbs that labour
   For not their fruit ;
By the foodless mouth with foodless heart for neighbour
   That, mad, is mute ;
By the child that famine eats as worms the blossom
   —Ah, God, the child !
By the milkless lips that strain the bloodless bosom
   Till woe runs wild. . . . '

The *Marching Song* is an exultant and hopeful rendering of the *Pilgrims*.

' We mix from many lands,
  We march from very far ;
In hearts and lips and hands
  Our staffs and weapons are ;
The light we walk in darkens sun and moon and star . . .

With us the winds and fountains
  And lightnings live in tune ;
The morning-coloured mountains
  That burn into the noon,
The mist's mild veil on valleys muffled from the
  moon. . . . '

The very ardour of the fighting re-

publican—is any left?—throbs through the
Halt before Rome.

> 'March to the tune of the voice of her,
>   Breathing the balm of her breath,
>   Loving the light of her skies.
>   Blessed is he on whose eyes
>   Dawns but her light as he dies;
>   Blessed are ye that make choice of her,
>   Equal to life and to death.' . . .
>
>   . . . Only her bosom to die on;
>   Only her heart for a home,
>   And a name with her children to be
>   From Calabrian to Adrian Sea
>   Famous in cities made free
>   That ring to the roar of the lion
>   Proclaiming republican Rome.'

There is a quieter and sweeter beauty
in the poem called *Siena*, the town 'set
in the sand's red sea,' with its memories
of St Catherine.

> 'From the war-worn wastes without
>   In twilight, in the time of doubt,
>   One sound comes of one whisper, where
>   Moved with slow motions of slow air
>   The great trees nigh the castle swing
>   In the sad-coloured evening;

E

' *Ricorditi di me, che son*
La Pia"—that small sweet word alone
Is not yet gone.'

Many of the poems in this book after the lapse of thirty years require a historical commentary. A few require even an explanation of their purport.

The volume considered as a whole is perhaps somewhat cold, and probably does not add much to the world's system of philosophy or ethics. One can hardly imagine a revolutionary being inspired or instructed by the *Songs before Sunrise*. But for its torrent-like utterance, its enormous command of metrical effects and the peculiar distinction of each individual poem, it must be ranked among its author's highest achievements in the art of poetry. Its sustained loftiness of thought, its cold brilliance of light, not less than its writer's unapproachable power over rhythms, render it distinct from all other literature of the kind.

Any attempt at detailed criticism of the tremendous historic drama of *Bothwell* would be beyond the scope of this volume. Its conventional five acts run to the unconventional length of five hundred and thirty-two pages of about thirty lines apiece, from which even a critic with historical learning, uninterrupted leisure and exemplary patience might be justified in shrinking. By the happy reader endowed with leisure and patience, perhaps Darnley's narration of his dream,

Bothwell, 1874.

> ' And ever she that sat on the sea-rock
>   Sang, and about her all the rocks were white
>   With bones of men whose souls were turned to fire,'

and his passionate outcry before his death, the long speech of John Knox in the fourth act and the final speech of Mary will be accounted the best things in the book. The interest of the play is historical rather than poetic. Only the historian who has the details of Mary Stuart's career at his fingers' ends is competent to appreciate the dramatic ingenuity of condensation and selection exhibited in this volume and the subsequent play of *Mary Stuart*, but the gigantic volume has a continuous vigour of style for the mere unlearned reader of poetry to admire and enjoy.

The volume entitled *Songs of Two Nations* includes the *Song of Italy*, a hymn of praise in honour of Mazzini, originally published in 1867 ; an *Ode on the Proclamation of the French Republic* after the fall of Napoleon III. ; and a few sonnets under the name of *Dirae*, principally relating to the Italian struggle for independence from the rule of Austria. It is, as it were, a supplement to the *Songs before Sunrise*, and an acquaintance with the volume is necessary to complete one's knowledge of the poet's political opinions.

Songs of Two Nations, 1875.

Of Swinburne's second tragedy in imitation of the Greek manner I am reluctant to speak. It contains some of his finest writing, and yet to me it

Erectheus, 1876.

seems devoid of proper poetic feeling. It is full of splendid rhetoric, and yet it is productive of no emotion but pain.

The story of the play runs as follows. To Erectheus, King of Athens, hard pressed by Thracian invaders, the Pythian oracle has sent the message that Chthonia, child of Erectheus and Praxithea, must die for the salvation of the city. Chthonia is sacrificed and the invaders are beaten back.

Perhaps to others more credulous or tolerant of Greek superstition the sacrifice of Chthonia for the sake of Athens may seem a laudable thing. Possibly if the play were represented on the stage the horror of the crime would be diminished; but as read it is unendurable. Whether it is because the subject is inherently undramatic, or that the salt of human tears is wholly absent and the writer insists overmuch upon the extent of the sacrifice made by Chthonia of love for death—whatever the reason may be, the play has never seemed to me anything but 'fierce and barren' and intolerable.

So far from softening the horror of the barbarous murder of Chthonia, the writer has even accentuated it. The chorus of old men, * which begins

' Who shall put a bridle in the mourner's lips to chasten
  them,'

is ferocious, while the very beauty of the presence of Chthonia and of her words renders the central idea of the play more unendurable.

' That I may give this poor girl's blood of mine
 Scarce yet sun-warmed with summer, this thin life
 Still green with flowerless growth of seedling days,
 To build again my city ; that no drop
 Fallen of their innocent veins on the cold ground
 But shall help knit the joints of her firm walls
 To knead the stones together, and make sure
 The band about her maiden girdlestead
 Once fastened and of all men's violent hands
 Inviolable for ever . . .

      And the men,
 Mine unknown children of unsounded years,

---

* It is perhaps worth while to mention here that the chorus of *Atalanta* is a chorus of girls.

My sons unrisen shall rise up at thine hand,
Sown of thy seed to bring forth seed to thee,
And call thee most of all most fruitful found
Blessed; but me too for my barren womb
More than my sisters for their children born
Shall these give honour . . .'

Undoubtedly it is a triumph for a dramatist to make his audience feel deeply the grief or joy of his puppets, but in this case the dramatist succeeds only in making us feel a tearless anguish and a voiceless resentment.

For a Greek scholar, the construction of the play and the scheme of the choral metres possess an unusual interest. The tragedy is more perfect in form as an imitation of Greek models than *Atalanta*, particularly in the matter of the division of the choruses into strophe, antistrophe and occasionally epode. A consideration of the choral metres would demand a pamphlet to itself. Possibly the finest is that which relates the rape of Oreithyia by the Thracian god—

' Out of the north wind grief came forth,
    And the shining of a sword out of the sea,'

a rendering into words of the very force
and strength of the storm-wind. The most
tremendous certainly is that which describes
the long impending battle in action.

'καὶ μὴν ἔργῳ κοὐκ ἔτι μύθῳ
χθὼν σεσάλευται.'

But where Aeschylus is content with a
few words, Swinburne puts forth all his
strength.

'With a trampling of drenched red hoofs and an earth-
    quake of men that meet,
Strong war sets hand to the scythe, and the furrows
    take fire from his feet,
Earth groans from her great rent heart, and the hollows
    of rocks are afraid,
And the mountains are moved and the valleys as waves
    in a storm-wind swayed.
From the roots of the hills to the plain's dim verge and
    the dark low shore
Air shudders with shrill spears crossing, and hurtling
    of wheels that roar.
As the grinding of teeth in the jaws of a lion that foam
    as they gnash
Is the shriek of the axles that loosen, the shock of the
    poles that crash. . . .'

The description of the battle fought in a

thunderstorm, placed in the mouth of the Athenian herald, is a passage of fine rhetoric.

> 'The word
> Quick on his lips yet like a blast of fire
> Blew them together, and round its lords that met
> Paused all the reeling battle; two main waves
> Meeting, one hurled sheer from the sea-wall back
> That shocks it sideways, one right in from sea
> Charging, that full in face takes at one blow
> That whole recoil and ruin, with less fear
> Startle men's eyes late shipwrecked; for a breath
> Crest fronting crest hung, wave to wave rose poised,
> Then clashed, breaker to breaker; cloud with cloud
> In heaven, chariot with chariot closed on earth,
> One fourfold flash and thunder.'

The most dramatic point of the play has been well seized by the writer, in the simple words of the reply of Praxithea to the messenger who brings news of the death of Erectheus—

> 'I praise the gods for Athens.'

That the harshness of the central motive of the tragedy had occurred to the dramatist would seem probable from the introduction at its close of Athena herself—*dea e machina*—with consolatory words. But there are some who refuse nevertheless to be comforted, for whom still and forever

> 'A cry goes up from the ghost of an ill deed done
> And a curse for a virgin slain.'

After the harshness of *Erectheus* the sense **Poems and** of relief is almost divine with **Ballads.** which one turns again to pages **Second** **Series, 1878.** wherein the master has been content to be neither politican nor patriot, but a poet.

The poems of the second series of *Poems and Ballads*, though less passionate, less tumultuous, than those of the first, possess a finer maturity, a nobler strength, a more splendid restraint. The tranquillity, the statuesque dignity of some of the finest poems in this book have not been matched by the later utterances of their author.

The serenity of a sunset pervades the

noble poem *In the Bay*, written to the memory of Marlowe, but even finer and more majestic are the incomparable verses, *Ave atque Vale*, in memory of Charles Baudelaire. However little the poet of *Les Fleurs du Mal* may seem to have in common with the poet of *Poems and Ballads*, his strange and melancholy spirit appears to have possessed a strong fascination for the younger writer.

'Thou sawest, in thine old singing season, brother,
  Secrets and sorrows unbeheld of us :
  Fierce loves and lovely leaf-buds poisonous
Bare to thy subtler eye, but for none other
  Blowing by night in some unbreathed-in clime ;
  The hidden harvest of luxurious time,
Sin without shape, and pleasure without speech ;
  And where strange dreams in a tumultuous sleep
  Make the shut eyes of stricken spirits weep ;
And with each face thou sawest the shadow on each,
  Seeing as men sow men reap.'

On both men the resuscitation of the legend of Tannhäuser by Wagner seems to have produced an enduring effect, for the memory of Baudelaire's pamphlet on the music-poem again brings to the author of

Laus Veneris the memory of the diabolic goddess celebrated by him of old :—

'. . . That obscure Venus of the hollow hill,
  That thing transformed that was the Cytherean,
    With lips that lost their Grecian laugh divine
    Long since, and face no more called Erycine. . . .'

The intense *ennui* and loathing of life which inspired the greater part of the poems of Baudelaire are so antagonistic to the ebullient genius of Swinburne that perhaps the poem ought not to be read as a criticism of the *Fleurs du Mal*. But it is a superb tribute to an unforgettable man. The verses are carved as out of black marble, and possess a sonorous majesty, 'deep-chested music,' a little unusual in Swinburne.

Like its forerunner, this volume contains many poems which must be passed over without name in favour of a few. The incommunicable magic and music of *A Forsaken Garden*, full of the breath of dying summer, the perfume of falling rose-petals, the sadness of fading love, make the poem linger long in the memory.

None who have ever taken into their hearts the cadences of these divine ten stanzas can live but that now and again some remembrance of that ghost of a garden fronting the sea at the sea-down's edge must rise to their lips and eyes.

' Not a flower to be pressed of the foot that falls not ;
    As the heart of a dead man the seed plots are dry ;
From the thicket of thorns whence the nightingale calls not
    Could she call, there were never a rose to reply.
Over the meadows that blossom and wither
    Rings but the note of a sea-bird's song ;
Only the sun and the rain come hither
    All year long.'

The lovers who laughed or wept there ' a hundred sleeping years ago,' whose loves faded as roses or the rose-red sea-weeds or remained to the end, what of them ?

' All are at one now, roses and lovers,
    Not known of the cliffs and the fields and the sea.
Not a breath of the time that has been hovers
    In the air now soft with a summer to be.
Not a breath shall there sweeten the seasons hereafter
    Of the flowers or the lovers that laugh now or weep,
When as they that are free now of weeping and laughter
    We shall sleep.'

And the garden itself, earth, stones and thorns, must at last come to the same end.

'Till the slow sea rise and the sheer cliff crumble,
  Till terrace and meadow the deep gulfs drink,
Till the strength of the waves of the high tides humble
  The fields that lessen, the rocks that shrink,
Here now in his triumph where all things falter,
  Stretched out on the spoils that his own hand spread,
As a god self-slain on his own strange altar,
  Death lies dead.'

Almost equally beautiful is *A Wasted Vigil* with its exquisite pictures of a seaside dawn and the bitterness of its unrevealed tragedy.

'Couldst thou not watch one hour with me? Behold,
  Dawn skims the sea with flying feet of gold,
With sudden feet that graze the gradual sea;
  Couldst thou not watch with me? . . .

Sunbeam by sunbeam creeps from line to line,
Foam by foam quickens on the brightening brine;
Sail by sail passes, flower by flower gets free;
  Couldst thou not watch with me? . . .'

There is a deeper note in the poem *At a Month's End*, a companion piece with the *Félise* of the earlier volume, but possessing a maturer strength, a wider knowledge than the former poem. It is almost a novel in a few stanzas, but with the use of suggestion in the place of the usual statement of fiction. There is a curious similarity between this poem and the more recent novel of the Italian D'Annunzio, *Il Trionfo della Morte*. The 'sleek black pantheress' of the poem is an idealised version of the Ippolita of the later novel; more inconstant, perhaps, but for all intents the same woman.

> ' Strange eyes, new limbs, can no man give her ;
>   Sweet is the sweet thing as it is.
> No soul she hath, we see, to outlive her ;
>   Hath she for that no lips to kiss ?
>   .   .   .   .   .
>
> For a new soul let whoso please pray,
>   We are what life made us and shall be.
> For you the jungle and me the sea-spray,
>   And south for you and north for me.'
>   .   .   .   .   .

The lover of the poem, however, is luckier than he of the novel, for he escapes with his life.

> ' But I who leave my queen of panthers,
>   As a tired honey-heavy bee
> Gilt with sweet dust from gold-grained anthers
>   Leaves the rose-chalice, what for me ?

From the ardours of the chaliced centre,
   From the amorous anthers' golden grime,
That scorch and smutch all wings that enter,
   I fly forth hot from honey-time.

But as to a bee's gilt thighs and winglets
   The flower-dust with the flower smell clings;
As a snake's mobile rampant ringlets
   Leave the sand marked with print of rings;

So to my soul in surer fashion
   Your savage stamp and savour hangs;
The print and perfume of old passion,
   The wild-beast mark of panther's fangs.'

There is a keener sense of natural beauty in this book than is shown in the earlier poems — the natural beauty of earth as opposed to the sea. The *Vision of Spring in Winter* is full of the longing that the weary dweller in towns has in the dreary winter months of rain and mud for the expected and long-delaying English spring.

' O tender time that love thinks long to see,
   Sweet foot of spring that with her footfall sows
   Late snowlike flowery leavings of the snows,
Be not too long irresolute to be;
O mother-month, where have they hidden thee?
   Out of the pale time of the flowerless rose

I reach my heart out toward the springtime lands,
  I stretch my spirit forth to the fair hours,
    The purplest of the prime ;
I lean my soul down over them, with hands
  Made wide to take the ghostly growths of flowers ;
    I send my love back to the lovely time.'

The same pure open air of natural things
—as opposed to the hothouse luxuriousness
of his earlier love-poems—shines here in
such a poem as the *Ex Voto* and in the
Four Songs of Four Seasons. The first
of these, *Winter in Northumberland*, is a
good example of Swinburne's power of
adapting and making perfect music of
metres over which earlier writers have
blundered and fallen.

      ' Through fell and moorland,
        And salt-sea foreland
        Our noisy norland
          Resounds and rings ;
        Waste waves thereunder
        Are blown in sunder
        And winds make thunder
          And cloud-wide wings ;
        Sea-drift makes dimmer
        The beacon's glimmer ;
        Nor sail nor swimmer
          Can try the tides

F

And snow-drifts thicken
Where, when leaves quicken,
   Under the heather the sundew hides.'

As clear and strong as the impression given in this poem of the sea–beaten and wind-swept Northumberland heights is the vision of *Spring in Tuscany*,

' Rose-red lilies that bloom on the banner ;
   Rose-cheeked gardens that revel in spring ;
      Rose-mouthed acacias that laugh as they climb,
Like plumes for a queen's hand fashioned to fan her
With wind more soft than a wild dove's wing,
      What do they sing in the spring of their time ? '

and of *Summer in Auvergne*,

' Dawn, as a panther springs,
   With fierce and fire-fledged wings
   Leaps on the land that rings
      From her bright feet,
   Through all its lava-black
   Cones that cast answer back
   And cliffs of footless track
      Where thunders meet,'

and of the desolate *Autumn in Cornwall*, by the steep and lonely cliffs of Tintagel, which have found mention more than once in the prose and poetry of Swinburne.

Those who have felt the inexplicable

charm of the melancholy north coast of Cornwall, the loveliness of the more radiant bays and capes of the Lizard, will be grateful to Swinburne for his praise and love of a country known little to those who can find no pleasure in scenes this side of the Channel.

> ' Tintagel and the long Trebarwith sand,
>   Lone Camelford and Boscastle divine
> With dower of southern blossom, bright and bland
>   Above the roar of granite-baffled brine ' *

have found an enduring place in his mind and work, but to the incomparable loveliness of Kynance Cove he has paid a tribute of words not too enthusiastic for the utter divinity and beauty of that wonderful bay which has yet found no painter or poet to reproduce in colour or words a hundredth part of its miraculous enchantment. Not even has the author of *Tristram of Lyonesse* succeeded in conveying into speech the effect of the colouring of that marvellous jewel of Nature.

---

* *Poems and Ballads*.   Third Series.   'In memory of John William Inchbold.'

A noticeable feature of this volume is to be found in the English and French poems written in memory of the French poet and critic Théophile Gautier, and reprinted here from the volume of memorial verses published in 1873, entitled *Le Tombeau de Théophile Gautier*. To that volume Swinburne also contributed a poem in Greek which has not been reprinted. The memory of Gautier has somewhat of the charm and fragrance which lives in the memory of Charles Lamb. He passed 'not crownless to Persephone,' and of his mourning wreath no flowers are fairer than these wound therein by his friend.

The translations from the French of François Villon—'Villon, our sad, bad, glad, mad brother's name' is the refrain of Swinburne's ballad to that unlucky and splendid poet—are interesting, but the marvellous achievement of Mr John Payne's translation into verse of the whole of Villon, as it is a completer, is even a more noticeable feat than Swinburne's.

The very little information this poet has

Songs of the Springtides, 1880.

condescended to give his readers concerning his own personal affairs is to be traced only in this volume, *Songs of the Springtides*. To unlock his heart with a sonnet key, in the scornful phrase of Browning, has not been a habit of Swinburne's. The absurdity of regarding the dramatic lyrics of the early *Poems and Ballads* as the personal utterances of a lyrist was pointed out by their author in his reply to the assailants of his morality at the time of their publication. So far as one might judge from all preceding poems, their author has been fortunately exempt from the average sufferings of humanity. Such sympathy as leaps from the responsive memories of the readers of such poems as the sonnet of Keats which begins, 'Bright star, would I were steadfast as thou art,' or Shelley's stanzas *Written in Dejection near Naples* is a thing which Swinburne, as a poet, would, so it appears, have scoffed at rather than sought for. But in this volume there are a few traces of feeling not so utterly removed from common humanity as is the greater bulk of his work.

> ' In fruitless years of youth dead long ago
> And long beneath their own dead leaves and snow
> Buried, I heard with bitter heart and sere
> The same sea's word unchangeable nor knew
> But that mine own life-days were changeless too
> And cold and fierce and barren . . .'

Yet, even after the slight confession of the average tendency of 'youthful poets' to 'melancholy,' the speaker in this poem, *On the Cliffs*, turns on himself almost in anger for his former participation in mortal weakness.

Of the three poems in this volume, the first, called *Thalassius*, is in some measure an idealised autobiography, a spiritual poet's progress. As portion of it has been included in the published 'Selections' from Swinburne's poems, it is presumably valued highly by its writer. The finest passage in it is a transcription into words of the famous painting of Titian—the riot of the 'Maenad and the Baccharid'—but more terrible than the jocund revelry of the painted Bacchus and his train. To a certain extent this poem is a lengthier recapitulation of the prelude to the *Songs before Sunrise*.

The poem called *On the Cliffs* is to my mind a poem of considerably more value and interest than *Thalassius*, and is, in addition to its poetic worth, a sufficiently luminous criticism of the Lesbian poetess beloved alike of Catullus and Swinburne. It was no doubt written for the purpose of including a translation of a few of the actual words of Sappho which have come down to us. The speaker of the poem is clearly the writer himself, and the scenery described may well have been that of the shore of the Undercliff.

'Between the moondawn and the sundown here
 The twilight hangs half starless. . . .
 But higher the steep green sterile fields, thick set
 With flowerless hawthorn even to the upward verge
 Whence the woods gathering watch new cliffs emerge
 Higher than their highest of crowns that sea-winds fret,
 Hold fast, for all that night or wind can say,
 Some pale pure colour yet,
 Too dim for green and luminous for grey.'

It is to the watcher on such a coast at twilight that the words of the immortal poetess seem to storm the 'fortressed rock of silence,' to 'make all the night one ear.'

> ' *O thou of divers-coloured mind, O thou*
> *Deathless, God's daughter subtle-souled*—lo, now,
> Now too the song above all songs, in flight
> Higher than the day-star's height,
> And sweet as sound the moving wings of night!
> *Thou of the divers-coloured seat*—behold,
> Her very song of old !—
> *O deathless, O God's daughter subtle-souled !*
>
> .   .   .   .   .   .
>
> *Child of God, close craftswoman, I beseech thee*
> *Bid not ache nor agony break nor master,*
> *Lady, my spirit*—
> O thou her mistress, might her cry not reach thee?
> Our Lady of all men's loves, could Love go past her,
> Pass and not hear it?'

The Garden of Cymodoce which follows is an ode to the island of Sark with its memories of Victor Hugo. The volume concludes with a lengthy *Birthday Ode* to the same writer.

Published in the same year as *Songs of*
Studies in *Springtides* and the *Study of*
Song, 1880. *Shakespeare*, the intervening volume called *Studies in Song* goes nigh to
founder beneath the weight of the *Song
for the Centenary of Walter Savage Landor*
with which its bows are laden. So far from
being a song, this poem is an interminable
species of ode comprising fifty stanzas of
sixteen lines each, and covering, with its
annotations, sixty-five weary pages of print.
From the author's point of view it may
have seemed worth writing: from the point
of view of an average reader not blessed
with much patience or leisure, the 'song'
does not appear likely to repay a close
study of its purport. For the majority of
people Landor's dialogues are sufficiently
dull; but this summary in verse of Landor's
writing is very much duller.

The following translation into English
of the 'anapæstic heptameters' of the
Grand Chorus of Birds of Aristophanes
in a similar metre, with the addition only
of rhymes and double rhymes, is ingenious

enough and has no doubt an added interest for a Greek scholar.

The swimming song, entitled *Off Shore*, possesses a blithe strain of music, a clear sense of the passionate charm of the sun and sea, with

> ' Its wild-weed forests of crimson and russet and olive
>   and gold,'

seen far below the surface of the bright water,

> ' When the might of the summer
>   Is most on the sea ;
> When the days overcome her
>   With joy but to be,
> With rapture of royal enchantment, and sorcery that
>   sets her not free.'

All dactylic forms of verse in the English tongue the poet has declared to be unnatural and abhorrent, yet the dactyls of *Evening on the Broads* seem fitting enough for their subject, the slow fading of the ' colours and clouds of the twilight' over the ' shadowless waters' and 'the sterile wastes and waves of the land.'

'Inland glimmer the shallows asleep and afar in the
  breathless
  Twilight: yonder the depths darken afar and asleep.
Slowly the semblance of death out of heaven descends
  on the deathless
  Waters: hardly the light lives on the face of the
  deep.'

The long, soft lines of the poem palpitate
with the palpitant, dallying breath of the
twilight hovering and descending over the
'lapsing land' and the dusky broads until the
advent of the stars and the final triumph
of night. This is the finest poem of the
book.

The three sonnets on the busts of Nero
in the Uffizi Galleries of Florence, called
The Emperor's Progress, are in turn devoted
to the three stages of the 'child of brighter
than the morning's birth,' the youth with
the weary frown, the man 'beyond all men
most miserable' whom

'The loathsome bitterness of life
Leaves fearful of the bitterness of death.'

Companion pieces with these verses are
the sonnets on *The Launch of the 'Livadia,'*

the steam-yacht of the Czar Alexander II.,
'gold and fair marbles and again more
gold,' but 'rigged with curses dark' in the
affixed phrase of Milton.

' All curses be about her, and all ill
    Go with her ; heaven be dark above her way,
    The gulf beneath her glad and sure of prey
  And wheresoe'er her prow be pointed, still
  The winds of heaven have all one evil will . . .

                         . . . Hope be far
  And fear at hand for pilot oversea,
    With death for compass and despair for star
    And the white foam a shroud for the White Czar.'

The poem is dated in September 1880.
In March of the following year Alexander
expiated a few of his crimes with his own
life in a more startling fashion than by
drowning.

The series of poems entitled *By the North
Sea*, which conclude the volume, is a series
of impressions of the Suffolk Marshes.

  ' A land that is lonelier than ruin ;
    A sea that is stranger than death :
  Far fields that a rose never blew in,
    Wan waste where the winds lack breath ;

> Waste endless and boundless and flowerless
>> But of marsh blossoms fruitless as free :
> Where earth lies exhausted, as powerless
>> To strive with the sea.'

The spirit of those 'miles on miles on miles of desolation' rises before one as one reads.   Here is a clear impression of a landscape in that 'pale and troubled' land.

> ' Tall the plumage of the rush-flower tosses,
>> Sharp and soft in many a curve and line
> Gleam and glow the sea-coloured marsh-mosses
>> Salt and splendid from the circling brine.
> Streak on streak of glimmering sea-shine crosses
>> All the land sea-saturate as with wine.'

Strange too is the picture of the church-yard collapsing into the sea, the tombs, 'with bare white piteous bones protruded,' crumbling, sliding downwards and being swallowed by the waste of waves. The triumphal chant to the sun which closes the book is in clear, bright contrast with this picture of weariness and decay.

The principal interest of the concluding
Mary Stuart, 1881. volume of the story of the Queen
of Scots, like that of *Bothwell*, is
historical rather than poetic. The poet's
breadth of style carries him easily over a
considerable space of not very poetic
historical matter, but it is not until he
breaks away from the clogged back-waters
of history and trusts himself to the stream
of his own invention that the play becomes
actually dramatic.

The suggestion that the death of
Chastelard, twenty-five years before, and
the hand of Mary Beaton, should be the
things which brought Mary to the execu-
tioner's block is as poetic as it is just,
even if it be unwarranted by knowledge.
It completes and perfects the trilogy, like
the last touch of colour, the final chord or
rhyme. In this piece of poetic justice the
poet has a perfect success. The 'famous
and terrible letter' which Mary, 'with many
gracious excuses and professions of attach-
ment' wrote to Elizabeth repeating the
slanderous reports retailed concerning Eliza-

beth by 'Bess of Hardwick,' otherwise the
Countess of Shrewsbury, and did not
send, is in the play retained by Mary
Beaton, and being forwarded by her to
Elizabeth in revenge for Mary's forgetfulness of Chastelard, impels the English
queen, then wavering between the pardon
or death of Mary, to the signature of
the death warrant. The short scene, but
the best in the play, in which Mary com-
mands Mary Beaton to sing, and she
sings an old song of Chastelard's, is in
the sweet vein of the former beautiful
dramatic poem.

God, says Mary Beaton, aside,

'Prompts me, being most just,
To know by trial if all remembrance be
Dead as remorse or pity that in birth
Died, and were childless in her: if she quite
Forget that very swan-song of thy love,
My love that wast, my love that wouldst not be,
Let God forget her now at last as I
Remember: if she think but one soft thought,
Cast one poor word upon thee, God thereby
Shall surely bid me let her live: if none,
I shoot that letter home and sting her dead.
God strengthen me to sing but these words through
Though I fall dumb at end for ever. Now . . .

' Après tant de jours, après tant de pleurs
　Soyez secourable à mon âme en peine.
　Voyez comme Avril fait l'amour aux fleurs ;
　Dame d'amour, dame aux belles couleurs,
　Dieu vous a fait belle, Amour vous fait reine.

' Rions, je t'en prie ; aimons, je le veux.
　Le temps fuit et rit et ne revient guère
　Pour baiser le bout de tes blonds cheveux,
　Pour baiser tes cils, ta bouche et tes yeux ;
　L'amour n'a qu'un jour auprès de sa mère.

　　MARY STUART. Nay, I should once have known
　　　　　that song, thou sayest,
　And him that sang it and should now be dead :
　Was it—but his rang sweeter—was it not
　Remy Belleau ?

　　MARY BEATON. My letter—here at heart ! (*aside*).'

The concluding scene of the execution,
like that of Chastelard, is not witnessed
from the stage, but is described by a
witness.

The long narrative poem of *Tristram of Lyonesse* stands high in the list of Swinburne's works for sustained strength of expression and purpose. Whatever place may be awarded to the poem among the narrative poems of the world, it must be said that Swinburne has in his treatment of the particular subject outwritten the only other two English poets, so far as I remember, who have touched on the same subject. The magnificent ancient legend was disfigured not less by the objective prejudice of Tennyson than by the stupid doggerel of Matthew Arnold.

Tristram of Lyonesse, 1882.

Swinburne has lifted the moral tone of his poem above the divorce-court atmosphere in which Tennyson attempted to place the story of the love of Tristram and Iseult, and he has not—need it be said?—indulged in the slipshod inanities of Arnold's tuneless jingle. His triumph over such competitors was easy enough in this particular matter. But this elaboration and revivification of the ancient legend has to undergo one other comparison—namely, with the *Tristan und*

Isolde of Wagner. The intense dramatic interest of Wagner's music-poem, the absorbing and entrancing beauty and passion of its multitudinous and miraculous harmonies, are absent from the poem of words. In each direction the poet was at a disadvantage ; in the form of narrative verse, which admits of no great dramatic interest, and in the mode of human speech, which is below the capacity of many instruments for the expression of emotion. In some points the treatment of the story by Wagner and Swinburne is alike, in others it is dissimilar. The story of Tristram was dealt with by Wagner much as were the broken fragments of Siegmund's sword by his son : he made no attempt to weld the pieces together : they had to be molten and reforged before the perfect blade was worthy of the hand of Siegfried. Swinburne, on the other hand, has followed the legend more closely, though he has given a more prominent place than of old to the second Iseult. The Tristrams of Wagner and Swinburne are akin in their nobility and courtesy, but Swinburne's pro-

tagonist is a much saner and less excitable
lover than Wagner's, and he has an unfortunate tendency to prolix metaphysical mus-
ings.   Swinburne's Iseult is to me veiled
and shadowy, almost colourless, beside the
Isolde of the music-poem, passionate in all
things as a storm-wind, in vengeance, in
love, in death, but his portrait of the second
Iseult, the maiden-wife, is far clearer, and
makes an excellent piece of character-
drawing.

Here are the first lines of the poem :—

'About the middle music of the spring
  Came from the castled shore of Ireland's king
  A fair ship stoutly sailing, eastward bound
  And south by Wales and all its wonders round
  To the loud rocks and ringing reaches home
  That take the wild wrath of the Cornish foam,
  Past Lyonesse unswallowed of the tides
  And high Carlion that now the deep sea hides
  To the wind-hollowed heights and gusty bays
  Of sheer Tintagel, fair with famous days.'

There is no hatred or love between the
knight and the bride he brings from Ireland
to his Uncle Mark at the commencement of

this story, and the love-potion is drunken by them unwittingly. There are several excellent fights in the poem, after the manner of Sir Thomas Mallory, passages of adventure and many beautiful sea-paintings. The episode of the maiden marriage is gracefully and delicately handled, although the necessity of a revision of the ancient story is not apparent. The morality of the different episodes of the poem is somewhat complicated, and to my mind the morality of the whole would have been made more acceptable by the complete omission of any attempt to reconcile an antique fable with a modern virtue. The introduction of the religious question of sin in the vigil of Iseult at Tintagel is discordant. There is no artistic or moral error committed either by Dante or Wagner, in the damnation by one of the lovers, in their apotheosis by the other. From a religious point of view they were rightly damned, from a poetic they were rightly transfigured. But if, as it appears, Swinburne's Tristram is intended to be conscious of ' sin,' his treatment of his wife does not in my humble opinion seem to be of service in the mending of matters, but rather to make bad worse. The chief glory of the poem, however, lies in its descriptive passages, as, for instance, that of the Cornish coast and of Kynance Cove,

> 'The very bay whence very Love
> Most meetly might have risen, and most divine
> Beheld and heard things round her sound and shine
> From floors of foam and gold to walls of serpentine,'

or of the Queen's bower, where

> 'Far and fain
> Somewhiles the soft rush of rejoicing rain
> Solaced the darkness, and from steep to steep
> Of heaven they saw the sweet sheet lightning leap
> And laugh its heart out in a thousand smiles,
> When the clear sea for miles on glimmering miles
> Burned as though dawn were strewn abroad astray,'

or of Tristram swimming

> 'Between the live sea and the living sun.
> And mightier grew the joy to meet full-faced
> Each wave, and mount with upward plunge, and taste
> The rapture of its rolling strength, and cross
> Its flickering crown of snows that flash and toss

> Like plumes in battle's blithest charge, and thence
> To match the next with yet more strenuous sense.'

The book is full of beauty and sea-air, and the long, rhythmic swell of its rhymed verses seems born of the sonorous, limitless roll of the Cornish waves, breaking everlastingly on the black cliffs. There is not much if any pathos in Swinburne's version of the story. In it Tristram is not killed while he sits harping before Queen Iseult, as he is in the story of Mallory followed by Tennyson, but dies of his wounds before the ship which brings Iseult to him arrives, as in the version of Thomas of Brittany. Yet the pathos of the simple words of the old French chronicler is not captured by Swinburne. Iseult stands

> 'Above him newly dead
> And felt his death upon her: and her head
> Bowed, as to reach the spring that slakes all drouth;
> And their four lips became one silent mouth.'

The concluding lines of the poem which narrate the burial of the lovers at Tintagel glide into a strain of soft music.

' So came their hour on them that were in life
   Tristram and Iseult: so from love and strife
   The stroke of love's own hand felt last and best
   Gave them deliverance to perpetual rest . . .
   And these rapt forth perforce from earthly ground,
   These twain the deep sea guards and girdles round . . .

   . . . For the strong sea has swallowed wall and tower
   And where their limbs were laid in woful hour
   For many a fathom gleams and moves and moans
   The tide that sweeps above their coffined bones
   In the wrecked chancel by the shivered shrine :
   Nor where they sleep shall moon or sunlight shine
   Nor man look down for ever : none shall say,
   Here once, or here, Tristram and Iseult lay,
   But peace they have that none may gain who live,
   And rest about them that no love can give,
   And over them, while death and life shall be,
   The light and sound and darkness of the sea.'

Tristram of Lyonesse is undoubtedly a
fine and possibly a great poem, and yet its
author seems barely to have done himself
justice in it. The strength of the lyric and
dramatic poet seems hampered by the necessity of telling a story. But its multitudinous
beauties of detail and breadth of style render
it perhaps the fullest and finest fruit of his
maturity.

The narrative poem is followed in this book by a fine ode to Athens and a poem on *The Statue of Victor Hugo*.

The middle space of the volume is filled with sonnets for the most part on literary subjects, the record of the friendship of men and books. The keen interest which Swinburne has manifested in the events of the day, and his ever-responsive horror and loathing for the cruelties and tyrannies of the world, shine here in the sonnets which commemorate the assassination of the Czar Alexander in 1881,* and the Russian persecution of the Jews in 1882. To the twenty-one sonnets here included on *The English Dramatic Poets*, 1590-1650, should be added the sonnet on Cyril Tourneur which appeared in the second series of *Poems and Ballads*. The *Adieux à Marie Stuart* celebrate the conclusion of the trilogy dedi-

---

* Although this Czar has the liberation of the serfs to his credit, it should be remembered that he has the massacre and exile of tens of thousands of Poles, the murder and torture of thousands of his own subjects to the other side of his account. Assuredly in saying that no free man might for compassion rejoice at the termination of that despot's life, the poet was in error.

cated to the fame of the Queen of Scots, in
lines of perfect beauty.

> ' Queen, for whose house my fathers fought
>   With hopes that rose and fell,
> Red star of boyhood's fiery thought,
>   Farewell.
>
> They gave their lives, and I, my queen,
>   Have given you of my life,
> Seeing your brave star burn high between
>   Men's strife.
>
> .   .   .   .   .   .
>
> Farewell the song says only, being
>   A star whose race is run ;
> Farewell the soul says never, seeing
>   The sun.
>
> Yet, well-nigh as with flash of tears,
>   The song must say but so
> That took your praise up twenty years
>   Ago.
>
> .   .   .   .   .   .
>
> More bright than stars or moons that vary,
>   Sun kindling heaven and hell,
> Here after all these years, Queen Mary,
>   Farewell.'

The exquisite verses on children which
make up the rest of the volume are not
likely to suffer from any comparison with

any poet of children dead or to be, in spite
of their author's self-abasement before the
shrines of William Blake and Victor Hugo.
There is nothing sweeter or more fragrant
in English literature than the verses of this
poet in praise of babies and older children.
The 'deep truth that great poets are bi-
sexual' is not less deep than the truth that
whatever a woman may feel with regard
to children it has been left for men to
express all the charm and humour of baby-
hood and childhood. The thirty-one lyrics
in this volume, under the title of *A Dark
Month*, which chronicle the month's absence
of a child are flawlessly beautiful from beginning to end. From the poem called *A
Child's Battles* one or two stanzas may be
here transcribed, the best tribute to their
delightful humour and sweetness being a
humble refraint from commentary.

> ' We that would fain seem wise
> Assume grave mouths and eyes
> Whose looks reprove
> Too much delight in battle:
> But your great heart our prattle
> Cannot move.

We say, small children should
Be placid, mildly good
    And blandly meek :
Whereat the broad smile rushes
Full on your lips and flushes
    All your cheek.

If all the stars that are
Laughed out, and every star
    Could here be heard,
Such peals of golden laughter
We should not hear, as after
    Such a word.'

Swinburne has immortalised the childhood of this boy. In *A Child's Pity*, *A Child's Laughter* and *Comparisons*, and in the *Dark Month*, he has drawn a picture of childhood which will outlive the ages as it must by this time have outlived the boyhood of his friend.

There hangs about this volume a fragrance peculiarly its own, distinct from the impression produced by any other of the poet's books. There is an atmosphere of serenity and sweetness, of literary charm, not often found outside the pages of Charles Lamb. How full of the essential charm of books

are the lines which tell of the dreariness
caused by the absence of the child who
drank deep

> 'The golden vintage of Shakespeare, gleaming
>   In the silver vessels of Lamb.
>
> Our Shakespeare now, as a man dumb-stricken,
>   Stands silent there on the shelf:
> And my thoughts, which had song in the heart of them,
>   sicken
>   And relish not Shakespeare's self.
>
> And my mood grows moodier than Hamlet's even,
>   And man delights not me,
> But only the face that morn and even
>   My heart leapt only to see.'

The poet's prose tribute to Shakespeare
is dealt with hereafter, but as an example
of his catholicity of appreciation one may
select for passing mention his sonnet to
Dickens.

Whether the poet's tributes to the shades
of Wilkie Collins and Charles Reade were
more kindly and generous than critical is
a matter which need not be questioned here,
but the knowledge that the creator of
Boythorne and Skimpole is a favoured

friend of the author of *Poems and Ballads* is as satisfactory to the lovers of Swinburne as of Dickens. One may regret, however, that he has not paid a similar tribute to Thackeray, who is assuredly as worthy a subject for the critical pen of Swinburne as Dickens, and surely worthier than Reade or Collins.

The lightest and most delicate of Swinburne's volumes, the *Century of Roundels*, exhibits his skill in the art of verse no less than do his more important books. Each of these hundred roundels, wrought, in his own phrase, 'as a ring or a star-bright sphere,' is a jewel of perfect verse, 'round as a pearl or a tear.' The choice of one or two for a quotation is difficult, for no sooner is one selected than the remaining ninety-nine present their rival charms for notice. It is again a case of the phrase of Hugo beloved by the later poet: 'J'en passe et

A Century of Roundels, 1882.

des meilleurs.' The veiled griefs of *In Harbour* and *Recollections*, the regrets of *A Dead Friend* and *Past Days*, the flower-like tributes thrown on the grave of Richard Wagner, the baby-songs and child-songs, the flower-pieces and picture-pieces, the sketches of Guernsey and Sark, are all almost equally delightful and are all alike perfect. Here is a dexterous play on words, with a hint of deeper things, called *Chance*.

> ' But now life's face beholden
>   Seemed bright as heaven's bare brow
> With hope of gifts withholden
>   But now.
>
> From time's full-flowering bough
>   Each bud spake bloom to embolden
> Love's heart and seal his vow.
>
> Joy's eyes grew deep with olden
>   Dreams, born he wist not how;
> Thought's meanest garb was golden;
>   But now ! '

The two roundels on Rossetti's translation of Villon's roundel to Death have a personal flavour, but perhaps even more personal than these is the rhyme *To Catullus.*

'My brother, my Valerius, dearest head
  Of all whose crowning bay-leaves crown their mother
Rome, in the notes first heard of thine I read
    My brother.

No dust that death or time can strew may smother
Love and the sense of kinship inly bred
From loves and hates at one with one another.

To thee was Cæsar's self nor dear nor dread,
Song and the sea were sweeter each than other:
How should I living fear to call thee dead
    My brother?'

The roundel naturally lends itself more easily to lighter verse than to serious poetry, but in the hands of Swinburne it becomes capable of expressing thoughts and moods of deep feeling. The book is light and charming in its entirety, and as such affords a pleasant contrast with some of its companions.

For the sake of one more quotation from this volume, I may be permitted to transcribe the dedicatory roundel to the late Miss Christina Rossetti.

'Fly, white butterflies, out to the sea,
  Frail pale wings for the wind to try,
  Small white wings that we scarce can see
    Fly.

'Here and there may a chance-caught eye
  Note in a score of you twain or three
  Lighter or darker of tinge or dye.

'Some fly light as a laugh of glee,
  Some fly soft as a low long sigh:
  All to the haven where each would be
    Fly.'

After the roundel, the ballade. The nine

A Midsummer Holiday, 1884. beautiful poems which give the title to this volume and other subsequent poems are constructed on the old French form or on variations of it adapted to new metres at the author's will. One of the most charming of the *Midsummer Holiday* poems is that which is made to the honour of 'Our father Chaucer,' radiant with the breath of summer and the memory of the long dead poet. The quiet sketches of this series of poems, of the sea-strand, the 'low-pleached' country lanes, the mill-garden with its rows of sunflowers and beds of sweet-william, the flower,

' Held by love the sweeter that it blooms in Shakespeare's name,'

culminate in the exultant song of swimming, in the poet's best-beloved measure,

' The sea is awake and the sound of the song of the joy
of her waking is rolled
From afar to the star that recedes, from anear to the
wastes of the wild wide shore.'

with its refrain,

' Strike out from the shore as the heart in us bids and
beseeches, athirst for the foam.'

Following the ballades comes another long ode to Victor Hugo. The poem called *Les Casquets* deals with the terrible rocks of that name off the coast of Jersey. The poems to children, the impressions of Sark or English scenes, are charming, but after the actual poems of the *Midsummer Holiday* the most noticeable things in the book are the polemical or political verses of which a few seem to have been due to the agitation

H

connected with the rejection of the Franchise
Bill by the House of Lords.

> ' Clear the way, my lords and lackeys! you have had
>   your day.
> Here you have your answer—England's yea against
>   your nay:
> Long enough your house has held you: up, and clear
>   the way!'

Words written in the passion of the
moment are perhaps often better left un-
reprinted, but even the service done by
the House of Lords in stemming the tide
of the oratory of a later and more vicious
Cleon does not prevent approval of such a
taunt as this :—

> ' They are worthy to reign on their brothers,
>   To contemn them as clods or as carles,
> Who are Graces by grace of such mothers
>   As brightened the bed of King Charles.'

The three ironic sonnets on the ' clumsy
and shallow snobbery' of a journalist in
the *Saturday Review* of the 15th December
1883 are as finely indignant as the quoted
piece of newspaper writing is contemptible.
The Word for the Nation is as applicable

at the present day as it was at the time of its writing, with its scornful note of the cackle that

> ' We have not, alack, an ally to befriend us,
>   And the season is ripe to extirpate and end us :
> Let the German touch hands with the Gaul
>   And the fortress of England must fall,'

and its haughty knowledge that such cackle is no more than

> ' The tribute of rage and of rancour,
>   The tribute of slaves to the free,
> To the people whose hope hath its anchor
>   Made fast in the sea.'

I have spoken above of Swinburne's *Tristram of Lyonesse* as the finest and fullest fruit of his maturity. It would, no doubt, be to speak after the manner of the Hibernians if one were to say that the dramatic poem of *Marino Faliero* is even finer, and yet there would be much truth in the statement. As a poem *Tristram* is perhaps a greater achievement

Marino Faliero, 1885.

than *Faliero*, but in point of human interest
and expression of thought the later-published
play stands high above the narrative poem.
It is the most thoughtful, the most human
of all the great poet's great works. He has
kept himself well in hand throughout. He
has a subject eminently suited to his
opinions, and he has lavished on it his best
workmanship. To appreciate thoroughly
its splendid vigour, its strength of style
and wealth of verbiage, one must place
beside it Byron's uninspired abortion of
dulness on the same subject. Neither
play would in all probability have any
chance of success on the stage, but with
regard to the matter of writing and spiritual
interest of each a comparison of the two
plays is all but ridiculous. How ineffably
bad is the writing of Byron's play is in-
credible until one reads it. One falls then
on such lines as these :—

'You drew me from my honourable toils
  In distant lands—on flood, in fields, in cities—
You singled me out like a victim to
Stand crowned . . .'

or these :—

> ' The many-twinkling feet so small and sylph-like,
>   Suggesting the more secret symmetry
>   Of the fair forms which terminate so well.'

Beside the comparison of the actual writing of the two men, the comparison of scene with scene is possible and affords an interesting study, but one which cannot be gone into in this place.

Swinburne's study of the old Doge Marino Faliero ranks high among the dramatic creations of literature. He can be compared with no other or smaller creation than King Lear. He is perhaps more sinning and less sinned against than Lear : less foolish or optimistic he is as certainly as he is equally tempestuous and hot-headed. Like Lear too he is absolutely noble and high-minded. What the actual Faliero was or might have been had he succeeded in overthrowing the state of Venice is another matter. The principal moral difficulty of the actual story of Faliero—the fact that his sudden conspiracy against the state, his instantaneous desire for reformation, was due to a public insult to himself and his wife and the neglect of the Senate to punish the offender in a manner adequate to the Doge's anger—is cleared away by the dramatist, but a certain doubt rises again when the book is closed. That a powerful prince, who in a superstitious age was in his early days hot-tempered enough to knock down a bishop bearing the Host in his hands on the score of unpunctuality, should resent two public insults so far as to wish to overturn the offending constitution, and in so doing destroy a large number of his enemies, is natural enough. The motives of Swinburne's Faliero are almost too lofty to be credible if the play is transferred to actuality, but in reading it one's doubts are for the time assuaged. Faliero too had little time for aping a Cæsar.

''Tis seventy years since I was called a child,'

he tells his youthful Duchess. To his Lear she is almost Cordelia. Their relationship — neither altogether parental and filial, nor wholly marital—is beautifully and charmingly delineated. The sword of vengeance is placed in Faliero's hand rather than sought for by him, but at the moment when his triumph seems possible he requires more than vengeance—the resurrection of a fettered commonwealth.

'If these who have wronged me, being wiped out,
   May leave this Venice with their blood washed white,
   Clean, splendid, sweet for sea and sun to kiss
   Till earth adore and heaven applaud her—then
   Shall my desire, till then insatiable,
   Feed full and sleep for ever,'

are his words. On being offered a crown as first of citizens, in the name of citizens, he cries :—

                           'Good, my friend,
   The foulest reigns whence ever earth smelt foul
   When all her wastes and cities reeked of Rome
   Were by that poisonous plea sown, watered, fed :
   The worst called emperors ever, kings whose names
   Serve even for slaves to curse with, lived by vote
   And shone by delegation.'

The remaining characters of the play

are not given much importance. Faliero
fills the stage. Bertuccio is a milder edition of the tempestuous old noble. The
Duchess is an excellent young wife. The
rest of the characters complete the story
without possessing much individuality—
Steno, the Admiral, Lioni and others.
Lioni represents the better side of the
aristocracy of the Venice of the day as
Steno represents its worst, but his con-
servatism is ferocious enough. Speaking
to the traitor of Faliero's conspiracy, he
says :—

> 'Ye would
> Make ripe that harvest, fill that winepress full,
> Which now not fifty years from this, ye know,
> Dolcino thought to reap and tread, and bring
> Equal and simple rule of right again
> Among us called by Christ's name here on earth—
> And how he died remembering, inch from inch
> Rent living with red iron, and his bride
> Burnt limb from limb before his eyes.'

The first three acts have plenty of
dramatic movement, but the fourth and
fifth are practically a monologue on the
part of the Doge, broken by the chant of
the monks as he waits for the striking of

the bell of St Mark's, which is to be the
signal of the uprising, by the words of the
Senate when his revolution has fallen into
dust, and again by the monks' Latin hymn
as he waits for the noonday of his execution.
Here are a few lines from the latter part of
that superb soliloquy :—

                              'Seven years since
Mine old good friend Petrarca should have died,
He thought, for utter heartbreak, and he lives,
And fills men's ears and souls with sweeter song
Than sprang of sweeter seasons : yet is grief
Surely less bearable than death, which comes
As sure as sleep on all.   We deem that man
Of men most miserably tormented, who
Being fain to sleep can sleep not : tyrants find
No torture in their torturous armoury
So merciless in masterdom as this,
To hold men's lids aye waking : and on mine
What now shall fall but slumber ?   Yet once more,
If God or man would grant me this, which yet,
Perchance, is but a boy's wish, fain I would
Set sail and die at sea : for half an hour,
If so much length of life be left me, breathe
The wind that breathes the wave's breath and rejoice
Less even in blithe remembrance of the blast
That blew my sail to battle, and that sang
Triumph when conquest lit me home like fire—
Yea, less in very victory, could it shine

Again about me—less than in the pride,
The freedom, and the sovereign sense of joy,
Given of the sea's pure presence . . .
                              . . . Come,
Bring me but toward the landing whence my soul
Sets sail, and bid God speed her forth to sea.'

One may doubt whether these splendid lines, which have the sentiment or inspiration of the North Sea and the Atlantic rather than of the tideless Adriatic drifting between the Venetian houses, idling along the Lido, are quite applicable, but their beauty and nobility are beyond all question. The violence of Faliero in the first scene of the second act is somewhat harsh, but in all other respects the entire poem is harmonious. It is a masterpiece of literature.

The rhymed tragedy of *Locrine* partakes, **Locrine,** by virtue of its complicated metres, **1887.** rather of the nature of an amusement than of that of a serious piece of work. Its fundamental idea seems to have

been that a play could be written in different
varieties of rhymed metre without losing all
significance as a work of art. The idea
could hardly have occurred to any other than
Swinburne, and assuredly it could not have
brought forth so good a fruit if fostered and
tended by any other hands. Indeed, the
subleties of the rhymes seem well adapted
to the retelling of the ancient legend of
Sabrina, and the whole play is graceful
and charming. The love of Locrine for
Estrild his 'Scythian concubine,' 'a
strange-haired woman with sad singing
lips,' * and for his daughter Sabrina is simply
and delicately told, while the jealousy of
Guendolen, the lawful wife, the villainy of
Camber and the boyish prowess of Madan,
are equally well delineated.

The first scene of the first act is written in
the ordinary heroic couplets : the rhymes of
the entire second scene are strung together
on the plan of the sonnet. The system of
the second scene of the second act is the
ottava rima familiarised here by the use of it

---

* *Chastelard*, iii. 1.

by Byron in his *Don Juan*. The first scene of the third act is written in the metre used in the poet's *Laus Veneris*, but with each third line giving the principal rhymes for the following stanza after the fashion of the *terza rima*. The second scene of the fourth act is in *terza rima* proper. The concluding scene of the fifth act returns to the heroic couplet. The nomenclature and mysteries of the other scenes may be left to the curious reader.

Hampered in this fashion by a deliberately complicated method of writing, it is not surprising that the play, poetic and well wrought though it is, does not rise to any great height of inspiration or music. The most surprising thing about it is that under such trying circumstances it should be so well put together and readable, although a further proof of the poet's versatility and ability in handling metrical difficulties is not in itself a matter for astonishment. The play does not lend itself to quotation.

There is a curious contrast between the
Poems and first and third series of the volumes
Ballads. labelled *Poems and Ballads*. After
Third Series, a lapse of twenty-three years, the
1889. singer of abnormal loves has become the
lyrist of infantine charms, the republican
poet celebrates the success of a limited
monarchy, the erewhile wanderer in the
Horselberg and on Lesbian promontories
pens a *Ballad of Bath*. Yet the critic is
unwary who judges from these things that
the fire which inspired the earlier works is
extinct or dying: witness the righteously-
indignant lines with which the poet de-
nounced the infamy of Russian Government
once more laid bare in a recent account
of Siberia.

The two longest poems in this book, *The
Commonweal* and *The Armada*, were written
in commemoration of the fiftieth anniversary
of the Queen's accession to the throne and
of the three-hundredth anniversary of the
sea-victory known best by the title of the
poem just mentioned.

The sanity of the *Commonweal* is refreshing

to those who are a little weary of Swinburne's diatribes concerning the Third Napoleon, Victor Hugo and the French Republic in general. In fact, even the most ardent of republicans must find the French Republic of to-day a somewhat irritating *protégée ;* and there are signs that Swinburne's constant affection for that scolding mistress has grown thinner. The France that was 'glorious and blood-red, fair with dust of battle and deaths of kings' can now hardly seem from any political point of view other than a withered and wrinkled harridan given to screaming from toothless jaws incapable of biting. 'Not wholly vile' is the only compliment he is able now to pay that unfortunate land whose misfortunes are of her own seeking. But even in 1887, in the dark period of English internal dissension, Swinburne celebrated the event of the year in pure and stately verse.

'Eight hundred years and twenty-one
    Have shone and sunken since the land
    Whose name is freedom bore such brand

As marks a captive and the sun
 Beheld her fettered hand.

But ere dark time had shed as rain
 Or sown on sterile earth as seed
 That bears no fruit save tare and weed
An age and half an age again,
 She rose on Runnymede.'

It is worth remembering that it is a
republican, and not a royalist, who traces
lightly here the record of 'earth's lordliest
Commonweal' during the fifty years

'Since in a maiden's hand the sign
 Of empire that no seas confine
First as a star to seaward shone.'

The hope of universal peace with which
the record began ended in 'war upon war,
change after change': and yet the hope of
man's progress remains.

'As from some Alpine watch-tower's portal
 Night, living yet, looks forth for dawn,
 So from Time's mistier mountain lawn
The spirit of man, in trust immortal,
 Yearns toward a hope withdrawn.'

From what poet has England heard such

divine words of praise as these? Assuredly from none of her recent doggerel rhymsters.

> ' The sea divine as heaven and deathless
>   Is hers, and none but only she
>   Hath learnt the sea's word, none but we
> Her children hear in heart the breathless
>   Bright watchword of the sea.

.   .   .   .   .   .

> Each hour that sees the sunset's crest
>   Make bright thy shores ere day decline
>   Sees dawn the sun on shores of thine,
> Sees west as east and east as west
>   On thee their sovereign shine.

> The sea's own heart must needs wax proud
>   To have borne the world a child like thee.
>   What birth of earth might ever be
> Thy sister? Time, a wandering cloud,
>   Is sunshine on thy sea.'

The long poem—magnificent in spite of its defects—which in the following year acclaimed the anniversary of the Armada, would, in my humble view, have been yet more magnificent if its writer had exercised a little more restraint upon his religious animosities. In a poem such as this, a certain deference to the demands of popularity is advantageous. A ballad on the

Armada which might have been learnt by schoolboys and recited in public would have been a priceless gift. But it is to be feared that the chance of writing a poem which would have supplanted Macaulay's fragment in the hearts of schoolboys was lost by Swinburne; nor can it be said that in this poem is the blood kindled and the ears enthralled as they are by Tennyson from the first to the last notes of his superb ballad of *The Revenge*.

The atmosphere of the Elizabethan period as it has been learnt by English boys from Macaulay, and from Kingsley in *Westward Ho!* and from many a less distinguished romance, is curiously lacking here. To the average schoolboy the Papist of such stories is inevitably a traitor or a coward: it is only later that he thinks—if he has not given up thinking—of the possibility of prejudice. But the continual references to the Papist's God in this poem, in voluminous sarcasm, are unlikely to amuse the schoolboy, and, for myself, seem wearisome and out of place. It is the sea-fight

I

that we want, and not a theological diatribe. A single verse would have disposed of the religious side of the Armada. To a blatant Protestant this voluble blasphemy of the Romish Church might perchance be pleasing : to a blatant Atheist, certainly. But to a critic without a leaning toward any particular religion or irreligion it appears singularly unpleasant and ill-advised, and does suggest the utterance of the question whether the Protestant deity of Elizabethan England was a much kindlier or more tolerant being than that of the Spanish Church.

A far sweeter note is touched in the quiet verses which follow addressed *To a Seamew.*

> ' When I had wings, my brother,
>   Such wings were mine as thine :
> Such life my heart remembers
> In all as wild Septembers
> As this when life seems other,
>   Though sweet, than once was mine ;
> When I had wings, my brother,
>   Such wings were mine as thine.'

The consideration of this poem naturally induces a comparison between it and the two famous odes of Shelley and Keats. The buoyant, exquisite melodies of the *Ode to a Skylark*, fresh and clear and bright as a stream of water bubbling down a mountain-side in the sun, the rich, undertoned harmonies of the *Ode to a Nightingale*, are not matched by the less spontaneous and less ambitious music of Swinburne's rhymes. Yet as Shelley has identified himself with his lark, and the thought of Keats simultaneously recalls his 'light-winged Dryad,' so has Swinburne joined his poetry to the flight of the stronger and broader-winged bird.

> ' For you the storm sounds only
>   More notes of more delight
> Than earth's in sunniest weather ;
> When heaven and sea together
> Join strengths against the lonely
>   Lost bark borne down by night,
> For you the storm sounds only
>   More notes of more delight.'

As Shelley sighed for the gladness which inspired the overflowing rapture of the lark's song, as Keats desired the forgetfulness of the world's weariness and fever, so the later

poet craves for the unlimited freedom of the
sea-bird's flight.

> ' But thine and thou, my brother,
>   Keep heart and wing more high
> Than aught may scare or sunder;
> The waves whose throats are thunder
> Fall hurtling each on other
>   And triumph as they die;
> But thine and thou, my brother,
>   Keep heart and wing more high.
>
> .   .   .   .   .
>
> Ah, well were I for ever,
>   Wouldst thou change lives with me,
> And take my song's wild honey,
> And give me back thy sunny
> Wide eyes that weary never,
>   And wings that search the sea;
> Ah, well were I for ever,
>   Wouldst thou change lives with me.'

The rigorous restrictions of the metre
chosen are obviously prejudicial to the
chance of the poem rivalling the spontaneous freedom of Shelley's lyric, or the
easier capacity of Keats's ode; and in verses
not quoted here there is a frequent strain
to adapt the words to the rhymes. The
poem possesses neither the marvellous

melody of Shelley nor the wonderfully felicitous phrasing of Keats; but however much may be found wanting in the poem when compared with two such masterpieces of art, undoubtedly for sincerity and sweetness of utterance it must be held to be no unworthy companion to the earlier odes.

To pass over the many delightful poems in the volume—the verses to babies, sea-songs and memorial verses—without more mention than the title of the poem called *Neaptide*, is necessary in order to arrive the sooner at those in which the poet has achieved an unusual pathos. Of the nine poems in which he has gone back to the style and dialect of the old Border ballads, there are three which seem to me to be perfect in pathos—*A Jacobite's Farewell*, *A Jacobite's Exile*, and *The Tyneside Widow*. The *Jacobite's Farewell* must be quoted in its entirety.

> ' There's nae mair lands to tyne, my dear,
>   And nae mair lives to gie :
> Though a man think sair to live nae mair,
>   There's but one day to die.

> For a' things come and a' days gane
>   What needs ye rend your hair?
> But kiss me till the morn's morrow,
>   Then I'll kiss ye nae mair.
>
> O lands are lost and life's losing
>   And what were they to gie?
> Fu' mony a man gives all he can,
>   But nae man else gives ye.
>
> Our king wons over the sea's water,
>   And I in prison sair:
> But I'll win out the morn's morrow,
>   And ye'll see me nae mair.'

It would be difficult, I should imagine, to produce from any literature a poem of sixteen lines of such utter perfection of noble pathos. The home-sickness of *The Jacobite's Exile* is touched by an equally sympathetic hand, and the yearning of the exile as we read seems almost sadder than the quieter despair of the condemned prisoner. How utterly true are the touches of local colour, the love of well-known names that seem almost strange in a strange land!

> ' On Aikenshaw the sun blinks braw,
>   The burn rins blithe and fain:
> There's nought wi' me I wadna gie
>   To look thereon again.

On Keilder-side the wind blaws wide :
  There sounds nae hunting horn
That rings sae sweet as the winds that beat
  Round banks where Tyne is born.

       .   .   .   .   .   ,

But O gin I were there again,
  Afar ayont the faem,
Cauld and dead in the sweet saft bed
  That haps my sires at hame !

We'll see nae mair the sea-banks fair,
  And the sweet grey gleaming sky,
And the lordly strand of Northumberland,
  And the goodly towers thereby,
And none shall know but the winds that blow
  The graves wherein we lie.'

But however pathetic these poems may seem, *The Tyneside Widow* is the only one of the three, and indeed of all Swinburne's poems, which could not well be read aloud without bringing tears to the eyes of the reader and his hearers. The desolation of the widow, for whom the happiness of 'a' lovers' and the brightness of the 'sma' flowers' serve but to increase her sorrow, with her 'bairn down in the mools' and 'the father under the faem,' is too human and pitiful for any other sympathy than tears. The growing passion of the poem, the bitterness of happy things, are lost if it be not read as a whole, but it is better to transcribe four verses than to quote not at all.

> ' The bairn down in the mools, my dear,
>   O saft and saft lies she ;
>   I would the mools were ower my head,
>   And the young bairn fast wi' me, my love,
>   And the young bairn fast wi' me.
>
> The father under the faem, my dear,
>   O sound and sound sleeps he ;
>   I would the faem were ower my face,
>   And the father lay by me, my love,
>   And the father lay by me.
>   .   .   .   .   .
>
> We were weel fain of love, my dear,
>   O fain and fain were we ;
>   It was weel with a' the weary world,
>   But O, sae weel wi' me, my love,
>   But O, sae weel wi' me.
>
> We were nane ower mony to sleep, my dear,
>   I wot we were but three ;
>   And never a bed in the weary world
>   For my bairn and my dear and me, my love,
>   For my bairn and my dear and me.'

If the third series of *Poems and Ballads* is

not a match for its forerunners, the world would have been the poorer for its loss— and of how many books can we say the same thing? *The Commonweal* has an interest outside the circle of eternal art, but the three last poems I have mentioned possess as high an artistic value as any of Swinburne's earlier poems and a thousand times more pathetic charm of sorrow.

After an interval of three years the poet **The Sisters,** startled an unsuspecting world with **1892.** the publication of *The Sisters*, a play dealing with a love-tragedy in polite society at the beginning of this century. One may go far to seek for the reasons which prompted the poet of *Chastelard* to write and publish this domestic tragedy. Possibly the wish to produce something in a new manner, the weariness of a settled style, had something to do with the matter. Certainly the poet could not have written in a manner much more unlike his usual

manner, in a spirit less like his usual spirit.
At first sight the play looks like a burlesque
of Tennyson's early utterances, for here we
have two model English baronets for Tennyson's one, and two young men and two young
women who talk of dressing for dinner, the
library and the dinner-bell. But the play is
not a burlesque. It is a serious attempt to
write a tragedy in modern manners. So
anxious, indeed, has the writer been not
to exceed the limits of ordinary speech
that the actual tragedy of the play falls
flat, but much of the dialogue has a spice
of interest or amusement. If any judicious
relative in the early days of Swinburne's
existence ever expressed the hope concerning the productions of a young poet
—'deep in bloodshed'—uttered by one of
the model baronets of this play,

> 'Let us trust
> That happiness and age may make his Muse
> Milder,'

his faith in an almighty Providence has undoubtedly been justified. There was surely

nothing in the world more improbable in
1865 than that the author of *Poems and
Ballads* should some thirty years later
write a play largely imbued with schoolboy slang done into five-foot lines of this
kind.

ANNE

You stupid pair of schoolboys! Really, Frank,
You should not let him.

FRANK

                    I can't lick him, Anne;
We two—or you alone—might manage.

ANNE

                              Why,
The grooms must know he should not mount a horse
Yet.

REGINALD

    Would you never have me ride again
Because last year I got a fall?

ANNE

                              Appeal
    To Mabel.

REGINALD

        She was always hard on me.

MABEL

Always.

It is only fair to say that these are not the best lines in the book, but they are not the worst. The first love scene between Reginald and Mabel is even more portentous. Of course the Swinburne that we know appears occasionally—in the description of a pansy-bed, in a tirade concerning Wellington and Napoleon, in a glimpse of the Northumbrian moors and burns.

> 'Bright and tawny, full of fun
> And storm and sunlight, taking change and chance
> With laugh on laugh of triumph—why, you know
> How they plunge, pause, chafe, chide across the rocks
> And chuckle along the rapids, till they breathe
> And rest and pant and build some bright deep bath
> For happy boys to dive in, and swim up,
> And match the water's laughter.'

The swift, black tragedy of the interlude —the play within a play like that of *Hamlet* —rises for a moment to a more poetic style than that of its setting, but the final lines of the book which kill off two—if not three —of the actual characters collapse into a prostration of language incompatible even with domestic tragedy.

The play, however, considered as a whole, is not unamusing. It is not perhaps easy to admit the possibility of a reference in 1816 to Wordsworth by the young cornet or lieutenant—whatever his title may be—who bears the name of Reginald, although the point of his remark

> ‘Dear Anne,
> Don't you say “Frenchmen say”—say “Frenchmen lie,”

is even more obvious in 1900 than in 1816. Nor is it possible altogether to sympathise with the writer in regretting—or in regretting that one never experienced

> ‘Redgie’s old familiar friend, the birch,
> With all its blithe, lithe bounty of buds and sprays
> For hapless boys to wince at, and grow red,
> And feel a tingling memory prick their skins—
> Sting till their burning blood seems all one blush,’

with the same pathetic wistfulness of remembrance as seems to possess these lines.

The Sisters cannot be regarded as anything but the recreation of an idle hour of its author, but as such it has certainly a claim on the attention of his readers.

To speak at the present time of patriotic poetry is to call up a painful vision or remembrance of various and variously hideous attempts at verse much acclaimed by an illiterate populace. To say that any expression of Swinburne's on any political subject is of considerably more literary value than such stuff as fires the audience of a music-hall with enthusiasm is to say a totally unnecessary thing. But it is undoubtedly gratifying to find the true laureate of English poetry inspired with the same impulse that fills even such doggerel and its hearers with a proper sense of the place of England among the nations. It is not to Swinburne that the friends of dis-union and dismemberment, the worshippers of cowardice and treachery, may look for help. There was not much hope, perhaps, in 1894, when this book was published, of the overwhelming sense of duty to England which has since awakened and spread over an empire. But in the title-poem of this book, written 'after reading Sir Philip Sidney's *Arcadia*,' the poet wrote thus,

Astrophel, 1894.

addressing the memory of 'Sidney, lord of the stainless sword ':—

> 'But England, enmeshed and benetted
>   With spiritless villainies round,
> With counsels of cowardice fretted,
>   With trammels of treason enwound,
> Is yet, though the season be other
>   Than wept and rejoiced over thee,
> Thine England, thy lover, thy mother,
>   Sublime as the sea.'

In so black a season as that which followed the end of the reign of the demagogue whose energies were devoted to the internal disruption of Great Britain and to the external dishonour of her name, such a hope as is expressed in the verses just quoted, such a faith as shines in the lines below, from a poem entitled *England, An Ode*, seem almost heroic.

> 'All our past acclaims our future: Shakespeare's voice
>   and Nelson's hand,
> Milton's faith and Wordsworth's trust in this our chosen
>   and chainless land,
> Bear us witness: come the world against her, England
>   yet shall stand.'

It is not necessary to add the comment

that since these lines were written the witness has been borne.

In the poem *A Nympholept* — one of the finest of his later poems—the writer has gone back to and caught the spirit of paganism, weaving into his words the terror of the forests under a midsummer noon visited by the strange and terrible god, Pan, the rapture of the 'splendour of silence,' the 'delight of the perfect hour,' the perfume of earth under the 'naked noon,' the 'fearful charm of the strong sun,' the fear that turns to delight, the rapture that changes to the dread of the 'supreme dim godhead, perceived by the soul and conceived of the sense,' the vision of a form and a face, obscure and golden, growing great as the waxing moon, whose eyes 'embolden fear till it change to desire, and desire to delight.'

For sustained music and passion of utter- ance, this poem stands among the best of Swinburne's dramatic lyrics. His vision of nature as shown in this poem is not that of a modern, but that of an early

Greek poet. Such a poet as Wordsworth, who seeks sermons in stones, has another view of nature than that of the speaker of this poem, who calls on 'the gods hard by,'

> 'The divine dim powers
> Whose likeness is here at hand, in the breathless air,
> In the pulseless peace of the fervid and silent flowers,
> In the faint sweet speech of the waters that whisper there.'

Which of the two comes nearer to the great heart of nature is a matter for discussion elsewhere than in these pages.

There is nothing in the rest of the book so fine as the *Nympholept*. Such poems as *On the South Coast* or *Loch Torridon*, records of sea-side holidays, or *An Autumn Vision*, a tribute to Shakespeare's genius, included in a description of a marvellous sunset above a sullen sea, have a personal interest as well as the interest evoked by a study of their metrical achievements, but otherwise fall only into the second or third rank of Swinburne's poems. In his tribute to the memory of Grace Darling the poet

K

has a subject close to his heart. For the rest, the book comprises a number of elegiac poems to the memory of dead friends such as Sir Richard Burton, Philip Marston, William Bell Scott and Théodore de Banville — or of dead poets such as Robert Browning and Alfred Tennyson.

In one of the poems to Burton there is some fine word-painting of the 'wild and woful land' of Auvergne.

'The huddled churches clinging on the cliffs
    As birds alighting for a storm's sake cling,
Moored to the rocks as tempest-harried skiffs
    To perilous refuge from the loud wind's wing;

The stairs on stairs that wind and change and climb
    Even up to the utmost crag's edge curved and
    curled.'

The dexterous verses *To a Cat* are in a lighter tune than usual, recalling the gracility of Hugo and the love of Gautier for his long-haired friends.

In the *Tale of Balen* the poet has again

chosen a narrative subject, but in treating it somewhat in the manner of a lyric he has avoided the opportunity afforded of falling into the prolixity of certain passages of his *Tristram*. The choice of metre is a singular choice for a narrative poem ; it is that of Rossetti's *Burden of Nineveh*, but the poet has given it lightness and grace by dropping a single line from the second half of the stanza.

> ' Along the wandering ways of Tyne,
>   By beech and birch and thorn that shine
>   And laugh when life's requickening wine
>   Makes night and noon and dawn divine
>   And stirs in all the veins of spring,
>   And past the brightening banks of Tees
>   He rode as one that hears and sees
>   A sun more blithe, a merrier breeze,
>   A life that hails him king.'

This little artifice gives to the entire poem of two hundred and sixty odd stanzas an easy lightness and swing of movement. The poem, perhaps owing to its similarity of metre, suggests *The Lady of Shalott*, but it possesses none of the mincing preciosity of Tennyson's shorter and lighter poem.

The last volume of verse published by Swinburne up to the present time is the dramatic poem called *Rosamund, Queen of the Lombards,* founded on a story from Gibbon, which is too recent to call for further comment in this place.

Rosamund, Queen of the Lombards, 1899.

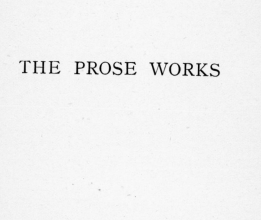

THE PROSE WORKS

THE PROSE WORKS

To be acquainted only with the poetic works of Swinburne is to be acquainted with but one half of his genius. In his poetry we find the singer of emotion and exaltation, but in his prose we find also the scholar and the critic. He has limited his capacity of learning and judgment to the province of poetry, but within that province—and it is a wide one—his breadth of knowledge is pre-eminent. To a complete knowledge of Greek, Latin, French and English poetry he has added a strength and suppleness of style, a command over language, equal to that of his verse. If his poetry had never seen the light of day, his critical studies would have given him an enduring place among English prose-writers. His prose is as distinct from all other prose as is his poetry. His style is unmistakable, and has varied, with his development, from the elaborate, pyrotechnic word-colouring of *Essays and Studies* to the more serviceable manner of the later *Miscellanies*. His criticism is emotional, and his views on men and things have in the course of his literary career undergone very violent changes. But in considering the mass of his critical work, it may be said without exaggeration that a more lucid critic, one with clearer insight and stronger power of expression of his opinions, has never lived. If any earlier English poet has been gifted with so fine a critical faculty as this, he has not used it : and one may doubt whether any critic of any literature has possessed so wide a knowledge, so strong a memory, or so keen an intuition as Swinburne.

His first piece of prose, after the publica-
Notes on
Poems and
Reviews,
1866. tion of the little story *Dead Love*
(1864), which has been already
mentioned, was polemical rather
than critical. The production of the *Poems
and Ballads* provoked a frantic outcry on
the part of the virtuous English press, to
which the poet, at the request of his pub-
lisher, made a brief and scornful rejoinder
in a pamphlet entitled *Notes on Poems
and Reviews*. The pamphlet, which is out
of print, cries for reissue. The style of it
is excellent, and it makes a singularly lucid
commentary on the methods and intentions
of the book of poems. To those reviewers
who attacked him as though for a personal
utterance he replied :—

'The book is dramatic, many-faced,
multifarious ; and no utterance of enjoyment
or despair can properly be assumed as the
assertion of its author's personal feeling or
faith.'

Without relaxing the contemptuous atti-
tude of the artist and seer for the ephemeral
journalist, the writer explains the birth of

such poems as *Anactoria*, *Laus Veneris* and *Dolores*, adding that he did not write for the young person, and asserting the right of the artist to a full expression of his art.

In 1868 the critic produced a volume of prose, which I believe is also out of print, concerning William Blake, the mystic poet and draughtsman. The book contained reproductions of some of Blake's designs.

William Blake, 1868.

The volume called *Under the Microscope*, now of great rarity, was designed as a reply to certain critics of Swinburne and Rossetti, including Mr Robert Buchanan, who had attacked his betters, under the pseudonym of Thomas Maitland, in an article entitled 'The Fleshly School of Poetry,' and a certain Mr Austin who may possibly be identifiable with the present Poet Laureate. The book, which

Under the Microscope, 1872.

is of some length, contains also a note on Whitman and Byron.

The poet's first volume of general literary
Essays and criticism, the *Essays and Studies*, a
Studies, collection of seven years' work, was
1875. published in 1875. It contains some
of the finest and most beautiful prose in our
language. At times, with all due deference,
I cannot but think that in the expression of
momentary or permanent loves and dislikes
he has in this and subsequent volumes
allowed himself to be carried out of the
proper depths of criticism. To express an
admiration or hatred is one thing ; to indulge
excessively in such expression is another. It
is possible that Louis Napoleon was the
most criminal of Frenchmen, it is possible
that Victor Hugo was the greatest of French
poets and the sincerest of patriots, but the
average English reader grows somewhat
restless and resentful under as much expatia-
tion upon their virtues and crimes as the

critic gives us. The sincerity of the critic's admiration for Hugo is not questionable, nor is it fitting for one with insufficient knowledge to question its foundation. For myself, however, I may confess that having followed from boyhood the critical lead of Swinburne, I have found disappointment but twice—in his judgment of Hugo and Landor. In their cases he has, so it seems, been compelled by his own admiration and by the growing indifference of others to an undue celebration of their causes. The volume of *Essays and Studies* commences with two essays on two books of Hugo—*L'Homme Qui Rit* and *L'Année Terrible*—and the last prose book published of Swinburne's closes with an account of Hugo's posthumous *Toute La Lyre*. Landor has not intruded so much into Swinburne's prose. The admiration of Swinburne for Hugo and for such a book as *L'Homme Qui Rit* is perhaps less astonishing than the splendour of words with which he has clothed that admiration and which render our disappointment doubly sharp as we turn from his words to the thing written of.

How disappointing it is, for instance, to turn from such a piece of splendid prose as includes the sentence which follows to the unspeakable female who figures in the book just named as *La Titane!*

'We seem to hear about her the beat and clash of the terrible timbrels, the music that Aeschylus set to verse, the music that made mad, the upper notes of the psalm shrill and strong as a sea-wind, the bull-voiced, bellowing under-song of those dread choristers from somewhere out of sight, the tempest of tambourines giving back thunder to the thunder, the fury of divine lust that thickened with human blood the hill-streams of Cithaeron.'

However short a distance one may be able to follow the admiration of Swinburne for Hugo, one must be glad that the admiration has given the critic an opportunity for such speech as this.

To Hugo the poet has been continuously faithful, but in many things, as we find from a study of his consecutive works, he has found it necessary to change his views.

The value of his critical opinion has increased with years, but his judgment at any time is valuable enough. The only claim which he would care to put up on behalf of the *Essays and Studies*, he writes, is ' That they give frank and full expression to what were, at the time of writing, my sincere and deliberate opinions. . . . I have desired above all things to avoid narrowness and dogmatism. . . . My chief aim, as my chief pleasure in all such studies as these, has been rather to acknowledge and applaud what I found noble and precious than to scrutinise or to stigmatise what I might perceive to be worthless and base.'

This laudable desire to praise has, however, led the critic upon ground where it is difficult for many to follow him. The praise of the long and beautiful essay, for example, upon the poems of Dante Gabriel Rossetti in *Essays and Studies* seems somewhat exalted for the subject. The writer is intoxicated with his own power over words, and scatters them broadcast like jewels, oblivious in the delight of colouring sentences of his duty as a critic. Who would have thought that some pages like this could have been begotten by the contemplation of the sonnet-sequence of the *House of Life?*—

'For something of these they must have to bring with them who would follow the radiant track of this verse through brakes of flowers and solitudes of sunlight, past fountains hidden under green bloom of leaves, beneath roof-work of moving boughs where song and silence are one music. All passion and regret and strenuous hope and fiery contemplation, all beauty and glory of thought and vision, are built into this golden house where the life that reigns is love; the very face of sorrow is not cold or withered, but has the breath of heaven between its fresh live lips and the light of pure sweet blood in its cheeks; there is a glow of summer on the red leaves of its regrets and the starry frost-flakes of its tears . . .'

This is a prose new to English ears, even though it wears a resemblance to that of Jeremy Taylor in its exalted eloquence, its pictorial colouring. Here is a marvellous sentence which could have been written by no man but Swinburne:—

'The song of Lilith has all the beauty and glory and force in it of the splendid creature so long worshipped of men as god or dreaded as devil; the voluptuous swiftness and strength, the supreme luxury of liberty in its measured grace and lithe, melodious motion of rapid and revolving harmony; the subtle action and majestic recoil, the mysterious charm as of soundless music that hangs about a serpent as it stirs or springs.'

The sentence coils and uncoils its long length as a snake may be presumed to do.

The essay on *Matthew Arnold's New Poems* (1876) includes a criticism of the critical—or rather the uncritical—essays of that poet which is completed in the note on Wordsworth and Byron in the *Miscellanies*. The perfect politeness of Swinburne's demolition of the uncritical positions thrown up by the poet who was transformed by the combined atmosphere of Rugby and Oxford into the likeness of a perfect prig is as amusing as it is subtle. But to the beauty of the best of Arnold's poems he pays a tribute as just as it is picturesque.

'His poetry is a pure temple, a white flower of marble, unfretted without by intricate and grotesque traceries, unvexed within by fumes of shaken censers or intoning of hoarse choristers; large and clear and cool, with many chapels in it and outer courts, full of quiet and of music. . . . In each court or chapel there is a fresh fragrance of early mountain flowers which bring with them the wind and the sun and a sense of space and growth, all of them born in high places, washed and waved by upper airs and rains. Into each alike there falls on us as we turn a consciousness of calm beauty, of cool and noble repose, of majestic work under melodious and lofty laws.'

The *Notes on the Text of Shelley* are for the most part what they purport to be, but the essay includes stray fragments of criticism and an interesting paragraph on the character of Count Cenci.

The essay on Byron in this book has been followed by a practical recantation on the part of its writer. The ear of Swinburne could not at any time have listened patiently to a Byron's 'feeble and faulty sense of metre,' but his impression at the date of this early essay that Byron 'rarely wrote anything worthless' and that he possessed 'the excellence of sincerity and strength' was not an impression that remained long in his mind. The essay, however, for all its half-hearted attempt at panegyric, and the unreason of the statement that the 'ancient name' of Byron would have been an impediment to 'a less strong man,' has a saner air of critical justice than the invective of the later article on the same subject.

The essay on John Ford is the precursor of the series of studies of the Elizabethan dramatists which make up a considerable portion of Swinburne's work in prose. His critical instinct has never been more acute and true than when he has written of the

old dramatists. He has taken up the task
of exposition of their work where Lamb
left it. He has indeed made them so much
his own, he has written so fully and finely
of their triumphs, with so wide a knowledge,
so perfect a critical instinct, that one might
be liable to forget that the very discovery
of the ancient worthies was due to the
servant of the East India Company. To
the ever-sweet and noble memory of Charles
Lamb Swinburne has paid due tribute,
and in amplifying the labour of love of his
forerunner he has acknowledged the debt
owed by all lovers of our literature to the
discoverer and first critic of the Eliza-
bethans. He has brought to the task not
a finer sense of criticism than Lamb, since
that were an impossibility, but he has
brought an ampler language and leisure,
and naturally the more indulgent hearing
which has been accorded to the critic with
so superb a record of poetic work than was
given to the unknown compiler of selections from the dramatic poets, has allowed
him greater liberty of space and freedom of

speech. No more vivid instance of Swinburne's critical faculty could well be chosen than the violent tirade in which he indulges in this essay with regard to Ford's play called *Love's Sacrifice*. The incident which is also the central motive of the play and here attracts the fiery anathematisation of the critic, is one which would not evoke from the majority of readers more than an incredulous shrug or a laugh. But the inartistic ugliness of it is to the acuter critic an absolute pain and worthy of a furious damnation.

The brief note on Coleridge is confined to a criticism of his verse, 'fluctuant and moonstruck as the sea is.' To his *Kubla Khan*, 'perhaps the most wonderful of all poems,' the critic gives his preference, *Christabel* and the *Ancient Mariner*, to borrow a metaphor, coming in second and third among the few competitors started in the race for the laurel-crown by that victim of opium and philosophy.

The two essays which conclude the volume — *Notes on Designs of The Old*

Masters at Florence and *Some Pictures of* 1868—exhibit the critic's interest in an alien art. In them he has attempted no pseudo-critical jargon of technical qualities: he has rather attempted to transfer into words the effect of designs and paintings seen in Florence and London, with excellent success. The verbal colouring of the essays bring the pictures clearly before one's eyes.

In the same year as *Essays and Studies* the writer also published a critical article on George Chapman, the Elizabethan dramatist and translator of Homer who brought such delight to the heart of Keats.

George Chapman, 1865.

The *Note on Charlotte Brontë* (1877) is self-explanatory and calls only for a brief comment here as practically the first evidence shown by the poet of an interest in another field of literary

Note on Charlotte Brontë, 1877.

art than his own. Since then he has given
other proofs of that interest in articles on
Emily Brontë, Charles Reade and Wilkie
Collins appearing in volumes referred to
later on.

The *Study of Shakespeare* (1880) is not
only the only satisfactory study of
the manner and style of Shakespeare which has seen the light,
but it shows the critic at his best both as a
perfect scholiast and an able interpreter.
An easy guide to Shakespeare it assuredly
is not. It is probably the most difficult
of commentaries to follow with a proper
understanding. It demands for full appreciation not only a more intimate acquaintance with Shakespeare than is usual
among readers unblessed with leisure or
a retentive memory, but also a sound knowledge of the other dramatists of the time.
The design of the book, he writes, ' Is
to examine by internal evidence alone the

A Study of Shakespeare, 1880.

growth and the expression of spirit and of speech, the ebb and flow of thought and style, discernible in the successive periods of Shakespeare's work.'

These periods he divides into three : the Lyric and Fantastic, the Comic and Historic, the Tragic and Romantic : the plays being placed in a sequence not determined by tradition or date of publication, but by the critical judgment of their order of production, after tracing and verifying 'the various shades and gradations of this progress, the ebb and flow of alternate influences, the delicate and infinite subtleties of change and growth discernible in the spirit and the speech of the greatest among poets.'

The commentary which accompanies this flowery path, tracing the gradual development of Shakespeare from the first discoverable touches of his hand in *Titus Andronicus* and *King Henry VI., Part I.*, through the historical plays and the comedies, to the tragedies and to the final romantic poems of *The Tempest*, the *Winter's Tale* and *Cymbeline*, is rich in thought and scholarship.

Assuredly none who have read and inwardly digested this volume can turn again to the actual words of Shakespeare without a sense of awakened appreciation, a keener insight, a stronger pleasure of understanding. If that is not the clearest proof of critical ability, the only aim and purpose of a critic, what is?

It is to be hoped that some future editor of Shakespeare may follow the arrangement of the plays here laid down, and include in his edition not only the *Arden of Feversham*, which it is 'not pardonable merely, nor permissible, but simply logical and reasonable to set down . . . a young man's work on the face of it, as the possible work of no man's youthful hand but Shakespeare's,' and the *The Two Noble Kinsmen*, the joint work of Shakespeare and Fletcher, which is omitted even now from the majority of editions.

In his note on the character of Hamlet, the critic disagrees with those who would make irresolution the 'signal characteristic' of the Prince of Denmark.

'The signal characteristic of Hamlet's inmost nature is by no means irresolution, or hesitation, or any form of weakness, but rather the strong conflux of contending forces.* That during four whole acts Hamlet cannot or does not make up his mind to any direct and deliberate action against his uncle is true enough; true, also, we may say, that Hamlet had somewhat more of mind than another man to make up, and might properly want somewhat more time than might another man to do it in; but not, I venture to say in spite of Goethe, through innate inadequacy to his task and unconquerable weakness of will; not, I venture to think in spite of Hugo, through immedicable scepticism of the spirit and irremediable propensity to nebulous intellectual refinement.'

The critic disclaims any intention of intruding upon the sacred ground of 'Gigadibs

---

* This is a curious slip of the pen, and perhaps the only loosely-constructed sentence in the whole of Swinburne. The meaning, taken with the context, is clear, but surely the writer overlooked the fact that a strong conflux of contending forces cannot be a characteristic of anyone's nature.

and the Germans,' of proving his perception of any point in the character of Hamlet 'unseized by the Germans yet,' but his reasoning that Hamlet's irresolution was due neither to 'half heartedness or doubt' or, may it be added, madness, is worthy of Teutonic or any other consideration.

Of *King Lear*, he writes :—

'It is by far the most Aeschylean of his works; the most elemental and primæval, the most oceanic and Titanic in conception. . . . We look upward and downward, and in vain, into the deepest things of nature, into the highest things of Providence ; to the roots of life, and to the stars ; from the roots that no God waters to the stars which give no man light ; over a world full of death and life without resting-place or guidance. But in one main point it differs radically from the work and the spirit of Aeschylus. Its fatalism is of a darker and harder nature. . . . Here is no need of the Eumenides, children of night everlasting ; for here is very Night indeed.'

In his judgment of Iago, however, that

'most potent demi-devil,' the critic's refinement upon the phrase of Coleridge
concerning 'Iago's motiveless malignity' is
unfortunately not exempt from a suspicion
that its super-sublety is to a large extent
due to the wish to include a sneer at Carlyle.

'Malignant as he is, the very subtlest and
strongest component of his complex nature
is not even malignity. It is the instinct of
what Mr Carlyle would call an inarticulate
poet. . . . He has within him a sense or
conscience of power incomparable, and the
power shall not be left, in Hamlet's phrase,
"to fust in him unused."'

But, putting aside this momentary doubt,
the 'closer than common scrutiny' which
the writer has given to 'this subtlest and
strangest work of Shakespeare's' goes deep
into the abysmal darkness of Iago's mind.

In choosing almost at haphazard a few
passages which suggest quotation, I have
been compelled to pass over many pages of
this luminous and delightful book not less
worthy of a complete and rapturous study.
To do more than point to the writer's sym-

pathetic and humorous 'appreciation' of Falstaff, his splendid rescue of the fat knight from the clumsy clutches of Victor Hugo ; his notes on Othello and Cleopatra ; his acute criticism of *The Two Noble Kinsmen*, dividing line by line the work of Fletcher from the work of Shakespeare ; his final 'salute of all my love' to 'the play of plays which is *Cymbeline*,' is unfortunately impossible.

I must add, however, to this too brief notice of the volume, the quotation of a few of its last words, not only for their own beauty, but as a warning to those who may deem in their ignorance that the vision of this poet is limited to the Faustines and Félises of his early verses.

'The passion of Posthumus is noble and potent the poison of Iachimo ; Cymbeline has enough for Shakespeare's present purpose of "the king-becoming graces" ; but we think first and last of her who was "truest speaker" and those who "called her brother, when she was but their sister ; she them brothers, when they were so indeed." The very crown and flower of all her father's daughters—I do not speak here of her human father, but her divine—the woman above all Shakespeare's women is Imogen. As in Cleopatra we found the incarnate sex, the women everlasting, so in Imogen we find half glorified already the immortal godhead of womanhood. I would fain have some honey in my words at parting—with Shakespeare never, but for ever with these notes on Shakespeare ; and I am therefore something more than fain to close my book upon the name of the woman best beloved in all the world of song and all the tide of time—upon the name of Shakespeare's Imogen.'

In 1886 two prose volumes of Swinburne saw the light : one, *A Study of Victor Hugo*, a comprehensive critical study of the poetic achievements of the French poet ; the other, a large and heterogeneous collection

A Study of Victor Hugo, 1886.

of critical essays bound together under the
title of *Miscellanies*.

The latter volume contains critical work
as fine as any which has been ac-
complished by Swinburne. There
is perhaps no beauty in the book like the
beauty of the prose in *Essays and Studies*,
no passage in it which, apart from its critical
interest, can be quoted for the sake of its
style or colour as an example of prose as
beautiful as verse. But it is a riper,
stronger, wiser book than its predecessor,
the *Essays and Studies*. From the *Miscellanies* one derives the impression even
of a certain geniality, although such passages as might be selected for examples of
the writer's humour are on the face of them
filled with a savage irony. A kindly
humour, a tolerant appreciation of less
gifted or less fortunate workmen than himself, a grace of humanity, are things not
to be looked for in Swinburne. As

*Miscel-
lanies, 1886.*

Shelley's skylark was an unbodied joy, he is an unbodied intellect subject to continual irritation. The irritation is generally shared by his reader until he has by repeated reading accustomed himself to the strange atmosphere.

To attempt to condense the magnificent utterance of this volume would be an impossible task. The simple attempt to write a few pages of exposition is as ungracious a labour as would be an attempt to explain from a pailful of water what is the likeness of the sea. There are few names in the poetic literature of the world not mentioned in this volume, and so illuminated by a phrase, a page or a paragraph.

The verbal violence of much of the writing is not infrequently jarring, but on the other side of it we have to place such appreciative kindliness of good feeling as for instance pervades the *Notes on Charles Lamb and George Wither*. It is generally with astonishment that one discovers the admiration of Swinburne for a man and a spirit so dissimilar as Charles Lamb. And yet his phrase that, 'All men worthy to know him would seem always to have loved him in proportion to their worthiness,' is as true regarding Lamb's posthumous lovers as his actual friends.

'For all who love him the charm of that companionship is alike indefinable and incomparable. It pervades his work as with an odour of sweet old-world flowers or spices long laid by among fine linens and rare brocades in some such old oaken or cedarn cabinet as his grandmother might have opened to rejoice the wondering senses of her boyish visitor at "Blakesmoor."'

Of the contents of the volume—the *Short Notes on English Poets*—Chaucer, Milton and Spenser—which are shorter than one might wish, the *Century of English Poetry* which illuminates the period of Pope and Dryden, the short articles on Congreve, Collins, Landor and Emily Brontë, the review of the novels of Charles Reade, the two notes on the French minor poet, Auguste Vacquerie, the historical sketch of Mary Queen of Scots, the appendices con-

cerning an unknown play of Dryden and
the character of Mary Stuart—what can be
said but that every line—save perhaps those
of the notes on Vacquerie—is worthy of
study? Here and there one may dare to
disagree on a debatable point, but there is
surely none who would dispute the brilliance
of learning, of analysis, of expression shown
in this mighty volume of criticism.

The essays on *Wordsworth and Byron*
and on *Tennyson and Musset*, as they are
the longest are also the most noticeable.
The attack on the literary and moral character of Byron is one of the most astonishing
things in the English language. Goaded
apparently into a state resembling frenzy
by the foolish laudations of Matthew Arnold,
the critic has set himself the task of de-
molishing the position of Byron both as a
poet and a man. Perhaps the only thing
one can say of this sustained onslaught is
that it is too overwhelming for its subject.
It creates a tempest when a puff of derision
would have been sufficient. The praise of
Matthew Arnold was sufficient to damn

Byron to all eternity : the attack of Swinburne serves to make one wonder whether there might not be something in Byron after all which necessitated the extent of this battle array. The demolition of Byron as a poet is complete enough, however. Of Byron's really strong point, the 'province outside the proper domain of absolute poetry' in which he 'was supreme—a king by truly divine right'—the critic has written with full appreciation, if only by way of emphasising Byron's failure to be suzerain or anything else of importance in a more artistic kingdom. But apart from its critical value the article is an astounding piece of invective which stands almost alone in the world of criticism, and as a piece of magnificent writing stands far above the only article which approaches it as a matter of critical invective — Macaulay's essay on Montgomery. With the writer's attack on Byron as a poet we may cordially agree, but his references to Byron as a man rouse a certain feeling of resentment. Whatever his faults may have been, Byron who died at Missolonghi will always remain in our minds as a man by the side of the dreamer Shelley, the pedant Wordsworth and the sophist Coleridge. Assuredly neither Byron nor Keats can be taunted with the fault of unmanliness if certain phases of the life of Shelley are insisted on in as hostile a manner as Swinburne insists on the faults of these contemporaries of the author of *Epipsychidion*.

To return, however, to the essay. I have space only for the quotation of a few sentences by way of exemplifying the method of the writing.

'The most remarkable point in his pretentious and restless egotism is that a man capable of writing such bad verse should ever have been capable of seeing, even in part, how very bad it was; how very hollow were its claims; how very ignorant, impudent and foolish, was the rabble rout of its adorers. . . . On taking up a fairly good version of *Childe Harold's Pilgrimage* in French or Italian prose, a reader whose eyes and ears are not hopelessly sealed

against all distinction of good from bad in
rhythm or in style will infallibly be struck
by the vast improvement which the text
has undergone in the course of translation.
The blundering, floundering, lumbering and
stumbling stanzas, transmuted into prose and
transfigured into grammar, reveal the real
and latent force of rhetorical energy that is
in them : the gasping, ranting, broken-
winded verse has been transformed into
really effective and fluent oratory. A
ranter, of course, it is whose accents we
hear in alternate moan and bellow from
the trampled platform of theatrical mis-
anthropy : but he rants no longer out of
tune. . . . Of Shakespeare he always wrote
and spoke as the author of the vilest and
most pretentious dramatic abortions ever
misbegotten by dulness upon vanity, or by
egotism upon envy, might naturally have
been expected to speak. . . . His lava
kisses and his baby earthquakes ; his walls
which have scalps and pinnacle those scalps
(was ever such jolter-headed jargon heard
before, from Bedlam or Parnassus ?) in cloud

less thick than the confusion of such a chaos
of false images; his stormy nights that are
lovely in their strength as is—of all things
on earth—the light of a woman's dark eye,
or a dark eye in woman; his day that
dies like a dolphin; his "grocer's shop kept
by one Nightingale," as Landor ingeniously
expounded the long, insoluble conundrum
with which the *Bride of Abydos* confronts
all comers on the threshold . . . his ramp-
ing renegades and clattering corsairs . . .
vulgar and violent resources of rant and
cant and glare and splash and splutter . . .
this is not the broken gallop of rough vigour;
it is the sickly stumble of drivelling debility
. . . his drawling, draggle-tailed drab of a
muse, Iynx, the screaming wry-neck . . .'
etc., etc.

'Here be words,' which we are not
accustomed to meet in the general run of
critical essays. To cut out of their context,
as I have done, short phrases and sentences
is no doubt unfair to their author, but in
no other way can one glean a few straws
from this wide field of rhetorical invec-

tive by way of illustration of its entire
likeness.

It is noticeable that in the very midst
of his furious attack, the writer has time
to devote a page or two to the almost
forgotten memory of Crabbe, 'the simple
old provincial clergyman whose homespun
habit of obsolete and conventional style is
the covering of a rarer pathos and a riper
humour' than Byron's.

The remainder of the essay is devoted
to a swift but searching study of Wordsworth, in prose as serious and fine as the
earlier part of the essay was volcanic. I
can quote but one passage, a good example
of the critic's illuminant powers of phrase.

'There is nothing outside Aeschylus so
Aeschylean as the magnificent and daring
accuracy of the single epithet which brings
before us a whole charge of storming
breakers as they crowd and crash upon
each other. No type has ever so well
represented, none could possibly represent
so well, the furious confusion and the
headlong pressure of their onset, as that

one word which makes us hear and see, across wind and lightning, the very sound and likeness of the "trampling waves."'

To Swinburne it is 'the sublimity of tenderness' which is Wordsworth's 'distinctive and crowning quality.' One might have thought rather that it was his occasional and, as it were, almost accidental capacity for making language 'fall into folds of faultless verse' which would have elicited the critic's highest admiration. Be that as it may, here at least is a sober and scholarly study of Wordsworth, not by any means blind to his faults or deaf to his crimes in the manner of the professed Wordsworthians, but simply just and unprejudiced and full of noble praise where it is due.

The article on *Tennyson and Musset* commences with the memorable and hysterical panegyric of the *Rizpah* of the former poet. I say 'hysterical' since it can be given to few if any to share the emotion of this critic on the first reading of *Rizpah*, to experience 'the actual and intolerable anguish, the terror that here darkens and condenses into sheer physical pain and horror . . . the pang of piercing and dreadful compassion which cleaves as it were the very core of "the spirit of sense" asunder.'

Tragic and pathetic as the poem is, it can rarely produce an emotion as deep as that portrayed in the words just quoted, even upon a reader anxious to pluck the agony of these words from the poem itself.

Of the apparent fact that there ever was 'a hotly-contested question of poetic precedence between Alfred Tennyson and Alfred de Musset' I am glad to own myself ignorant. To Swinburne's statement that 'Four lines of *Rizpah*, placed in one scale of the balance of judgment, would send all the loveliest verse of Musset flying up in the other, to kick the beam and vanish,' might be well added the opinion that any four lines of Tennyson, Gautier or Baudelaire would produce the same effect. It was surely some reminiscence of the early influence of Musset on 'the innocent mind of ingenuous youth' which prompted the author of this essay to his extraordinary kindness towards the memory of the author of *Namouna*. If the 'moral tone' of Tennyson as regards the relationship of his men and women is not over-lofty, what can be said of such productions as *Rolla* or the *Confessions?* The charge of prurience against the author of *Mlle. de Maupin* may be debatable : but against Musset it is palpably true. His morality, artistically or literally considered, is that of the valet of the author of *Don Juan*.

But if the critic is unreasonably kind to Musset, he is here somewhat ungracious to Tennyson. The brief and—as he acknowledges—inexhaustive estimate of Tennyson in this essay is not among the most acceptable of Swinburne's opinions. It is doubtless more difficult to appreciate one's co-equals and contemporaries, even for the least prejudiced of critics, than those who are beyond the discords of the present. But if Swinburne has not perhaps done justice to the late Laureate's work taken in the bulk, he has given to stray portions of it praise and to spare.

With a quotation of such a passage of praise, I must end this inadequate note of a volume which is beyond criticism and beyond any praise but mute admiration of its strength, its learning and its style. The passage which follows recalls the earlier beauty of Swinburne's prose with an added power or sweep of expression.

'Many years ago, as I have always remembered, on the appearance of the first four *Idylls of the King*, one of the greatest painters now living pointed out to me, with a brief word of rapturous admiration, the wonderful breadth of beauty and the perfect force of truth in a single verse of *Elaine*—

"And white sails flying on a yellow sea."

I could not but feel conscious at once of its charm and of the equally certain fact that I, though cradled and reared beside the sea, had never seen anything like that. But on the first bright day I ever

spent on the eastern coast of England
I saw the truth of this touch at once. . . .
There on the dull, yellow, foamless floor
of dense, discoloured sea, so thick with
clotted sand that the water looked massive
and solid as the shore, the white sails
flashed whiter against it and along it as
they fled. . . . But he must have learned
the more splendid lesson of the terrors
and the glories of the Channel before he
caught the finest image ever given in his
verse—the likeness of a wave "green-
glimmering from its summit—"

           ' "With all
Its stormy crests that smoke against the skies." . . .'

The volume devoted to the study of
Ben Jonson's life-work is as just,
illuminant and thorough as the
book on Shakespeare. The critic's
estimate of Jonson is summed up in the first
three sentences of the book — excellent

*A Study of
Ben Jonson,
1889.*

examples in themselves of the writer's
methods of critical comparison.

'If poets may be divided into two exhaustive but not exclusive classes—the gods
of harmony and creation, the giants of
energy and invention—the supremacy of
Shakespeare among the gods of English
verse is not more unquestionable than the
supremacy of Jonson among the giants.
Shakespeare himself stands no higher above
Milton and Shelley than Jonson above
Dryden and Byron. Beside the towering
figure of this Enceladus, the stature of
Dryden seems but that of an ordinary
man, the stature of Byron—who indeed
can only be classed among the giants by
a somewhat licentious or audacious use of
metaphor — seems little higher than a
dwarf's.'

Apart from the actual criticism of Jonson's
plays, masques, poems and essays, the book
has not, for a reader unacquainted with
its subject, that interest which is possessed
by the *Essays and Studies* or *Miscellanies*.
One might, I think, read these volumes

with interest and some appreciation without having a full understanding of the
matters involved. This would not be the
case with the present book. It is only
now and again that such a passage as
that quoted appears, whilst the epigram
that 'a worse translator than Ben Jonson
never committed a double outrage on two
languages at once' stands alone.

To the work by which Ben Jonson is
best remembered the writer has done
ample justice, perhaps even at too great
a length. His comedies and his verses
are known to all possible readers of these
lines. But Jonson's *Discoveries*, his brief
essays or *obiter dicta*, are less known.
Swinburne, in an article occupying a
third of this volume, places them above
Bacon's essays 'in truth of insight, in
breadth of views, in vigour of reflection
and in concision of eloquence.' To myself
they appear to be the equal of Bacon's
in one point—dulness. That is a matter
which may be well put down to one's
own want of intelligence, and it certainly

does seem to one such unintelligent reader
that Montaigne—a writer, I believe, never
mentioned by Swinburne—is a more readable essayist than either Bacon or Jonson.
But when we have a sentence or two of
Jonson's containing undoubtedly a worthy
if questionable opinion, 'that no great
work, or worthy of praise or memory, but
came out of poor cradles,' thrust upon us
with these words, 'There are few finer
passages than that in Landor ; in other
words there can be few passages as fine
in any third writer of English prose,' then
the most humble of readers turns at last, and
would suggest that in the matter of English
prose, neither Jonson nor Landor have been
at any time worthy of the pleasure of un-
loosing the latchet of the shoes of that
obscure doctor of Norwich who wrote on
Urn-Burial and was named Sir Thomas
Browne.

The volume entitled *Studies in Prose and*
Poetry, published eight years after
Miscellanies, a similar volume containing ten short essays on general
literary subjects and eight articles on the
subject of Hugo's posthumous works, is a
slighter book than its forerunner.

There is much in the book which is, at
first, exasperating to a degree not attained
by a perusal of Radical newspapers or
'literary' journals. In the essay on *The
Journal of Sir Walter Scott*, for instance,
the critic has wish to accentuate the
character of Sir Walter by a reference to
the 'abject unmanliness' of Keats. The
usual tone adopted by Swinburne in writing
of that great and unfortunate poet is singularly prejudiced, and is very curious after
his own sonnets on the subject of the
publication of the love-letters of John
Keats.* The author of the *Ode to a
Nightingale*, unfortunate as he was in his
brief life, has been equally unfortunate in
his posthumous admirers and editors, but

* 'A Midsummer Holiday.'   *In Sepulcretis.*

that a man of so high a literary position as Swinburne can stoop so far as to moralise above the grave of Keats is incomprehensible. Assuredly there is no one from whom one would have less expected such a thing. One resents it less on behalf of Keats than on behalf of one's admiration of Swinburne. And when, *per contra*, we are asked to admire the character of Sir Walter Scott, we are sorely tempted to admit nothing in Scott that might not appear in the character of any blatantly prosperous *bourgeois* who was honest enough when he got into difficulties to attempt the payment of his debts. But save for such moments as these, the essay is pleasant, kindly and sympathetic, and would almost persuade one to attempt the task of reading the Waverley novels. The expression of his opinions is a thing the critic has always allowed himself in full measure, and one hesitates to accuse him of indulgence in paradox, yet when we light on such a sentence as this, it has at first sight almost the savour of a paradox :—

'The more we know of Byron and Bonaparte, the lower do they lie in the estimate of sane and honest men ; the more we know of Wellington and Scott, the higher do they stand and the clearer do they shine.'

Of course it is the moral character of each man that is referred to, but the point of view is curiously paradoxical.

The recollections of *Professor Jowett* are interesting, but their interest lies more in the writer's reminiscences of himself than in those which relate solely to the translator of Plato. The fact that the ' physical energy' with which Jowett would 'press up a hill-side or mountain-side—Malvern or Schehallion—was very agreeable and admirable to witness,' is amusing to the fancy of the portly pedagogue striving to keep pace with his younger and lighter-limbed companion. The brief references to Tintagel and St Michael's Mount and ' The unique and incomparable sublimity of loveliness which distinguishes the serpentine rocks and cliffs and slopes and platforms of of Kynance Cove from any other possible presentation of an earthly paradise' are charming enough, but all too brief.

The little personal confession that Swinburne once took part with Jowett in editing a 'Child's Bible' is quaintly curious, but not surprising if we remember the poet's evident familiarity with the 'Scriptures.'

There is much that is charming, and a little that is annoying, in these two essays, but their charms and irritations must be left to the reader. The following notes on Webster and Herrick sin only in their brevity. The essay on Beaumont and Fletcher is more exhaustive. The article entitled *Social Verse*, written round a collection of poems of the lighter kind, is— but for one ferocious passage — in the critic's lighter mood and includes (in prose) the only Limerick—so far as I know— printed by Swinburne, which I here transcribe into verse.

'There was a bad poet named Clough
  Whom his friends found it useless to puff,
For the public if dull has not quite such a skull
  As belongs to believers in Clough.'

The kindliness of the following note on the novels of Wilkie Collins will not, it is to be feared, keep alive in the minds of a later generation the recollection of the novelist. In passing, one may note the mirthful reference to Mr W. S. Gilbert's *Engaged.*

' Belinda and her Belvawney, Cheviot and his Minnie, rise up before the eyes of enraptured if incredulous fancy, in the light— or should we say limelight?—of inextinguishable and inexpressible laughter.'

In his note on the American Walt Whitman entitled *Whitmania*, the writer has given perhaps too much prominence to a wholly futile writer in conferring upon him the honour of a few pages of antagonistic criticism.

The ironic note entitled *Tennyson and Darwin*, which establishes the fact that the author of the *Origin of Species* was also the real author of *Maud* in a manner as satisfactory and sane as that which proves Bacon to have written the plays of Shakespeare, is amusing. But one cannot help feeling that the editorial hand which excised from the letter of Miss Celia Hobbes a passage concerning Tennyson in which her language 'becomes—to put it mildly—contumelious' might well have exercised a similar discretion over certain passages of his own work other than this essay.

In *Les Cenci*, the chief interest lies in the French prose of the writer. He elaborates a little the study of the character of Count Cenci portrayed in the tragedy of Shelley with which we became acquainted in the *Essays and Studies*. In the graceful and charming French tongue the utterance of Swinburne seems harder and harsher than in English, while the distinguishing qualities of his style disappear.

An inability to appreciate properly the enthusiasm of Swinburne for Hugo does not necessarily detract from the pleasure of following his prose annotations to the French poet. In one passage of the second half of this volume he fills up a space left blank by Hugo in words which make one profoundly thankful for the omission of

Hugo to visit the Lac de Gaube above Cauterets and astonished at the absurd humility of the close of the following sentence :—

'The fiery exuberance of flowers among which the salamanders glide like creeping flames, radiant and vivid, up to the skirt of the tragic little pine-wood at whose heart the fathomless lake lies silent, with a dark dull gleam on it as if of half-tarnished steel ; the deliciously keen and exquisite shock of a first plunge under its tempting and threatening surface, more icy cold in spring than the sea in winter; the ineffable and breathless purity of the clasping water in which it seems to savour of intrusive and profane daring that a swimmer should take his pleasure till warned back by fear of cramp when but half way across the length of it, and doubtful whether his stock of warmth would hold out for a return from the far edge opposite, to which no favour-ing magic can be expected to transport the clothes left behind him on the bank from which he dived ; the sport of catching and taming a salamander till it became the pleasantest as well as the quaintest of dumb four-footed friends ; the beauty of its purple-black coat of scaled armour inlaid with patches of dead-leaf gold, its shining eyes and its flashing tongue—these things, of which a humbler hand could write at greater length than this, would require such a hand as Hugo's to do them any sort of justice.'

The extraordinary humility of such a declaration—the writer's sincerity is never a thing admitting of a moment's doubt—is not less extraordinary than his marvellous lapses from prose set in so fine a key to phrases expressive of some patent or latent personal annoyance which are not worth the publicity of print. Thus, for instance, even the last paragraph of the book is disfigured by a startling and apparently uncalled-for reference to certain 'casual trespassers and transgressors who come down to the seaside with a view to indulgence in cockney or in puritan in-decencies.' The point of it is barely intelligible, and the ' trespassers ' in question seem to be unidentifiable. Then — after this spasmodic outburst — the book closes with a fine thought, nobly expressed, suggested by the abortive efforts of 'a Cowley, a Tupper, an Emerson, a Whitman.'

'But there is something which these liberators have somehow failed to attain : there is the sublime liberty of expression, the supreme perfection of utterance, which never has been and never will be attained except by workmen in words (as by workmen in any other more or less plastic material) who can understand, accept, embrace and rejoice in the rules and conditions of their art : content in the recognition and happy in the acceptance of that immortal and immutable instinct whose impulse is for law, whose passion is for harmony, and whose service is perfect freedom.'

EPILOGUE

I HAVE reached at last the limit of my labour of analysis or exposition of the mass of the prose and poetic works of the greatest living English poet, and in looking back over what I have written I feel only that I have left unsaid one half of that which ought to have been said. My best hope in closing these pages is that I may have made clearer for a few a path through the flowery underwoods of the poet's many and great achievements.

That Swinburne is the greatest poet or the greatest dramatist England has known is not a proposition I wish to put forward or should care to uphold. He himself who has written so well of Shakespeare would be the first to condemn such an opinion. But that he is the greatest artist in poetic

utterance who has written in the English
tongue is an opinion I am anxious to
maintain. I do not say that the music
of Milton's verse has not a deeper tone,
that Shelley has not a sweeter and keener
melody, that phrases of Wordsworth or
Keats do not go deeper to one's inmost
understanding; but this I do say that no
English writer has had a wider knowledge
of the involutions of literary craftsmanship
—a more extensive empire over the world
of verbal expression. He stands promin-
ently among the world's inventors of
metres for lyrical utterance. He has not
achieved so great a work as the unknown
inventor of the hexameter or as Marlowe,
the creator of blank verse. He has not
invented a form to match the sonnet in
popularity. But as an inventor of rhythms
and forms as incapable of others' use as his
own music is inimitable he stands alone.
One of his principal achievements of course
has been his adaptation of the anapæst
to the English tongue, but he has never
used any metre in earlier or ordinary use

without developing new qualities in it, without showing of what further change of beauty it was capable. The melody of his lyrical speech is equalled only by two English poets—by Shelley and by Coleridge. And yet not even Shelley has surpassed the continuity and strength of the music of the *Triumph of Time* or the verses to Whitman, while of Coleridge's best work there are but a few pages. Of the sea and the sea-wind he has written as has no other poet from the beginning of the world whose works have come down to us, and for a book of love-poems what shall one place beside the *Poems and Ballads?* The dominant emotion of all his work is a delight in existence; in his early work the delight of erotic emotion, in his later work the delight of action, as portrayed in *Tristram* or the plays, and the delight of the wind and sea and liberty.

At the close of the century, when it seems as if the day of poetry were also drawing to its end, the comparison of the one great poet who remains with those who have gone before inevitably arises— the comparison of Swinburne with Tennyson and Browning. The delightful and exquisite talents of Rossetti and Arnold can hardly be placed in the same rank as these save only by a wholly unreasonable partisanship and admiration. Considered simply as a master of music and poetic expression Swinburne is undoubtedly a greater writer than Tennyson or Browning, and yet the restrained perfection of Tennyson's style and the warmth and depth of Browning's humanity give them again an equal position with him. Each in his best point excels the others : none can, I think, be fairly placed on a higher level than his compeers. Of the three, Tennyson has the fewest faults. He wrote neither *Sordello* nor the *Song for the Centenary of Walter Savage Landor*, but on the other hand he wrote neither *Andrea del Sarto* nor *Atalanta*. Browning's technical faults are as many as the stones on the 'pebbled shore.' Swinburne's chief enemy has been his exceptional facility of utterance and impatience of restraint, which have led him now and again in his later years to a certain verbosity and a habit of repetition of the same phrases and rhymes. In Swinburne one finds never the tranquillity which is found in Tennyson and Browning and in a higher degree in Shakespeare. He has dealt always in emotion, but it is rarely the emotion remembered in tranquillity of Wordsworth's famous phrase. One may read the last words of Othello and be tranquil, absorbed in the manifold wisdom and strength of Shakespeare, but there is little of Swinburne's work that is not disturbing. He permits no repose to the mind of his reader. With the possible exception of Shelley, he has the most poetic temperament of any English poet, the temperament tradition attributes to the inspired singer—the exaltation of thought and imagination unknown in the crowd of the uninspired. He has done more for the exaltation of poetry and the study of poetry than either of the other two great poets born in this century, and his influence upon future generations must be greater than theirs. He has carried poetic expression a step further than it had been carried by any writer before him. In the age of Pope and Dryden there was none who dreamed of the possibilities of our language in the hands of a Shelley, and after Shelley none has done more for exploiting the further capacities of metre and rhyme than Swinburne. For full appreciation one must know him by heart. The subtleties of his music need declamation for the perfect understanding of its beauty. He is no such painter in words as Tennyson. The patience required for the elaboration and condensation of thought and colour which render the work of Tennyson so admirable is alien to his genius. The tone of the greater part of Swinburne's work is curiously un-English. At the very first sight of his work it is difficult to follow his meaning ; the style seems curiously constructed and involved. The sensation disappears after a time, but at first his language seems one which has to be translated. His genius was ripened under many alien influences—the Latin literature of the decadence, the Greek dramatists and lyrists, the Hebrew prophets, the French medieval scribes and rhymers. In later life, the English side of his temperament is more apparent.

But here I must take my leave of this book, the fruit of a long desire and of many hours. To write worthily of Swinburne one needs a command of language equal to his own. That this volume can add one petal or one leaf to his laurel-crown I cannot dare to hope, but if as a 'garland of a day' it may serve to express the gratitude of one recipient for his many gifts, for many delighted hours and days absorbed in the charm of the music and glory of his verse, in the strength and splendour of his prose, its purpose will be served. From any praise or dispraise the object of so much may well turn aside. Of laudation he may

indeed be satiated; to condemnation in-
different. Yet surely of all men should
one be most happy who living hears that
praise which can die not until the end of
time for the creations of his thought and
his hand. Upon his finest work time can
have no power to destroy, but the grace
of strengthening years must enhance its
beauty, making eternal that which was
born to a temporal world. What new
gifts may be given us by a poet who at
an age when the most of mankind have
achieved their lives, retains the physical
and mental vigour of youth we cannot
tell, but assuredly no sun rose in so brilliant
a dawn and shone through so splendid a
noon but set in a yet more glorious array
of purple and gold. His highest fame,
his highest power upon the world of
literature, have perchance not yet been
attained, but haply his greatest glory will
come with later and unborn generations
of men. For surely as long as the blood
burns with the ardour of its spring, as
long as youth dreams and loves and

sorrows and its heart leaps to the sound
of the music of metre, as long as the wind
lifts the spirit with the exaltation of liberty
and life, and the sea circles a land where
the English tongue is spoken or read, so
long must endure the honour and glory
of his fame.

APPENDIX

TITLES OF THE WORKS

'The Queen-Mother and Rosamund,' .	1860.
'Dead Love,'	1864.
'Atalanta in Calydon,'. . .	1865.
'Chastelard,'	1865.
'Poems and Ballads' (I.), . .	1866.
'Notes on Poems and Reviews,' .	1866.
'William Blake,' . . .	1868.
'Songs before Sunrise,' . .	1871.
'Under the Microscope,' . .	1872.
'Bothwell,'	1874.
'Essays and Studies,' . . .	1875.
'George Chapman,' . .	1875.
'Songs of Two Nations,' . .	1875.
'Erectheus,' . . .	1876.
'A Note on Charlotte Brontë,'. .	1877.
'A Note on the Muscovite Crusade,' .	1877.
'Poems and Ballads' (II.), . .	1878.
'Songs of the Springtides,' . .	1880.
'Studies in Song,' . . .	1880.
'A Study of Shakespeare,' . .	1880.
'Mary Stuart,' . . .	1881.
'Tristram of Lyonesse,' . .	1882.
'A Century of Roundels,' . .	1883.

'A Midsummer Holiday,'	. .	1884.
'Marino Faliero,	. .	1885.
'A Study of Victor Hugo,'	.	1886.
'Miscellanies,'	.	1886.
'Locrine,'	. . .	1887.
'A Study of Ben Jonson,'	.	1889.
'Poems and Ballads' (III.),	.	1889.
'The Sisters,' .	. .	1892.
'Studies in Prose and Poetry,'.		1894.
'Astrophel,' .	. .	1894.
'The Tale of Balen,' .	.	1896.
'Rosamund, Queen of the Lombards,'.		1899.

The foregoing list comprises the principal volumes published by Mr Swinburne. Several of them are out of print and difficult to obtain, but the new edition of the poet's works, which is in preparation, will, it is to be hoped, be complete.

A fuller account of the adventures of the early books and of many stray verses and pieces of prose will be found by the curious bibliophile in an alas! almost unobtainable and lengthy bibliography by Mr Wise, which was privately printed in 1897.

To the list above may be added the novel— *A Year's Letters by Mrs Horace Manners*, which appeared in *The Tatler* in 1877. It was understood that the poet had determined not to reprint *The Heptalogia or the Seven against Sense*, a volume of parodies which was published anonymously in 1880, but the supposition appears to have been based on no authority, and the volume will, it is gathered, be included in the forthcoming collected edition. It is amusing, but is somewhat savage in spirit.

The poets parodied are Tennyson, Browning, Whitman, Patmore, Lytton, Rossetti and Swinburne. The exaggerated awkwardness of Browning's utterance is possibly the best. The lines are certainly unreadable.

'Ah, how can fear sit and hear as love hears it grief's
　　heart's cracked grate's screech?
　Chance lets the gate sway that opens on hate's way and
　　shows on shame's beach
　Crouched like an imp sly change watch sweet love's
　　shrimps lie, a toothful in each.'

The writer's parody of himself, entitled *Nephilidia*, begins thus :—

'From the depth of the dreamy decline of the dawn
　　through a notable nimbus of nebulous noonshine,

Pallid and pink as the palm of the flag-flower that
  flickers with fear of the flies as they float,'

and ends with the following line :—

' Till the heart-beats of hell shall be hushed by a hymn
  from the hunt that has harried the kennel of kings.'

The book was no doubt written in haste
for an hour's amusement, but it does not
possess the light and graceful humour
necessary for a volume of parodies, and,
if reprinted, must seem somewhat out of
keeping with the nature of the real work
of its author.

THE END

Colston & Coy. Limited, Printers, Edinburgh.